Python Programming

Includes *Python for Beginners*

and *Python Advanced Programming*

by Kevin Lioy

directions contained within is the solitary and utter responsibility of the recipient reader. Under no circumstances will any legal responsibility or blame be held against the publisher for any reparation, damages, or monetary loss due to the information herein, either directly or indirectly.

Respective authors own all copyrights not held by the publisher.

The information herein is offered for informational purposes solely, and is universal as so. The presentation of the information is without contract or any type of guarantee assurance.

The trademarks that are used are without any consent, and the publication of the trademark is without permission or backing by the trademark owner. All trademarks and brands within this book are for clarifying purposes only and are the owned by the owners themselves, not affiliated with this document

Table of Contents

4

Python for Beginners - Introduction

This book divulges proven steps and strategies to help beginners learn Python Programming quickly and easily. It is designed to be a practical, step-by-step tutorial of essential Python programming concepts for self-learners from beginner to intermediate level.
It uses a straightforward approach that focuses on imparting the important ideas without the heavy programming jargon. Python, after all, is a language with simple and easy-to- learn syntax.

The book features various Python programs as examples as well as a concise explanation of the different aspects of Python Programming. By the time you finish the book, you will be equipped with the necessary skills to create useful and practical codes on your own.

Chapter 1: What is Python?

Python is a broadly utilized abnormal state programming language made by Guido van Rossum in the late 1980s. The language places solid accentuation on code intelligibility and straightforwardness, making it workable for software engineers to create applications quickly.

Like all high-level programming dialects, Python code looks like the English language which PCs can't get it. Codes that we write in Python must be translated by a unique program known as the Python mediator, which we'll need to introduce before we can code, test and execute our Python programs.

There are likewise various outsider instruments, for example, Py2exe or Pyinstaller that enable us to bundle our Python code into remaining solitary executable projects for the absolute most prominent working frameworks like Windows and Mac OS. This enables us to disseminate our Python programs without requiring the clients to introduce the Python translator.

Why Learn Python?

There are an enormous number of abnormal state programming dialects accessible, for example, C, C++, and Java. The uplifting news is all abnormal state programming dialects are fundamentally the same as each other. What contrasts is principally the sentence structure, the libraries accessible and how we get to those libraries. A library is essentially an accumulation of assets and pre-composed codes that we can utilize when we compose our projects. On the off chance that you learn one language well, you can without much of a stretch get familiar with another dialect in a small amount of the time it took you to get familiar with the primary language.

Probably you are new to programming, Python is an incredible spot to begin. One of the key highlights of Python is its effortlessness, making it the perfect language for fledglings to learn. Most projects in Python require extensively less lines of code to play out a similar undertaking contrasted with different dialects, for example, C. This prompts less programming mistakes and decreases the advancement time required. Also, Python accompanies a broad accumulation of outsider assets that broaden the abilities of the language. All things considered, Python can be utilized for an enormous assortment of undertakings, for example, for work area applications, database applications, organize programming, game programming and even versatile improvement. To wrap things up, Python is a cross stage language, which implies that code composed for one working framework, for example, Windows, will function admirably on Mac OS or Linux without rolling out any improvements to the Python code.

A portion of the highlights that you may like with Python include:

• An elegant sentence structure which will make the projects so natural to peruse. Python is anything but difficult to utilize so the program will work without a great deal of bugs. In the event that you are doing specially appointed programming assignments or model advancement since it functions admirably without issues with keeping up the program.

• Has an enormous library that will work with other programming undertakings, for example, evolving documents, scanning for content, and interfacing with web servers.
• Python is extremely intelligent. This makes it simpler for you to test out little bits of code to check whether they work. You can likewise package it with an improvement situation called IDLE.

• If you might want to grow the programming language, it is anything but difficult to reach out into different modules like C or C++. Python programming can be kept running on any unit including Unix, Linux, Windows, and Mac OS X.

• The programming is free. You won't need to pay anything to download and utilize Python in your very own life. you can likewise make alterations and redistribute this item. It is under a permit, however it is an open source permit so others can utilize it.

• Even however Python is a straightforward programming language, it contains some propelled highlights like rundown cognizances and generators.

• Errors can be gotten rapidly in this programming. Since information types are powerfully composed, when you combine types that don't coordinate, it will raise a special case for you to take note.

You can bunch the codes into bundles and modules if necessary. There is a wide assortment of essential information types that you can browse including word references, records, strings, and numbers.

Python has been around for more than 29 years now and since it is probably the least demanding code to figure out how to use, there have been many various codes composed utilizing the framework. Fortunately this framework is publicly released so the code is accessible for any software engineer to utilize. You can introduce the Python program in your very own framework and use it for your very own utilization. Regardless of whether you are utilizing the codes to complete off an item or to keep in touch with your very own portion codes, the library of Python is anything but difficult to utilize. The codes that you need will be introduced into the libraries and since the program has been around for a long tie, they are going to cover basically anything you desire from mechanizing your server to making changes to an image.

Since Python is so famous, the network for Python is really enormous. There are community with heaps of systems administration and workshops accessible for this programming items and bunches of spots you can visit, both on the web and disconnected, to pose inquiries or to study the program. You might need to consider looking at a couple of these spots on the off chance that you are a tenderfoot with Python as it can assist you with learning more and even to meet some new individuals.

In the event that you are keen on beginning with coding, Python is perhaps the best alternative that you can make. It is easy to begin on and since it will take a shot at a wide range of stages, it makes certain to take a shot at your PC. Since it is anything but difficult to peruse, you will see that coding doesn't have as a test and you can make your own, or gain from others in no time.

Advantages and Disadvantages of Python

Advantages or Benefits of Python

The Python language has differentiated application in the product improvement organizations, for example, in gaming, web systems and applications, language advancement, prototyping, visual depiction applications, and so forth. This gives the language several advantages over other ones utilized in the business. A portion of its points of interest are-

Broad Support Libraries

It gives huge standard libraries that incorporate the regions like string tasks, Internet, web administration devices, working framework interfaces and conventions. The greater part of the profoundly utilized programming errands are now scripted into it, so it limits the length of the code to be written in Python.

Incorporation Feature

Python includes the Enterprise Application Integration that makes it easy to build Web benefits by conjuring COM or COBRA segments. It has great control abilities as it calls legitimately through C, C++ or Java by means of Jython. Python likewise forms XML and other markup dialects as it can keep running on all cutting edge working frameworks through same byte code.

Improved Programmer's Productivity

The language has broad help libraries and clean item arranged structures that expand from 2 to 10 times the software engineer's profitability versus utilizing the dialects like Java, VB, Perl, C, C++ and C#.

Productivity

With its solid procedure joining highlights, unit testing system and upgraded control capacities contribute towards the accellerated speed for most applications and efficiency of uses. It is an extraordinary choice for structure versatile multi-convention organize applications.

Confinements or Disadvantages of Python

Python has changed profitable highlights, and developers lean toward this language to other languages since it is anything but challenging to learn and code as well. In any case, this language has still not made its place in some processing fields that incorporates Enterprise Development Shops. Along these lines, this language may not fathom a portion of the undertaking arrangements, and constraints incorporate

Trouble in Using Other Languages

The Python users become so familiar with its highlights and its broad libraries, so they face issue in learning or taking a try at other programming idioms. Python specialists may see the pronouncing of cast "qualities" or variable "types", syntactic necessities of including wavy props or semi colons as a burdensome undertaking.

Weak in Mobile Computing

Python has made its quality on numerous work area and server stages, however it is viewed as a frail language for versatile figuring. This is the explanation not many versatile applications are worked in it like Carbonnelle.

Gets Slow in Speed

Python executes with the assistance of a mediator rather than the compiler, which makes it delayed down in light of the fact that arrangement and execution help it to work regularly. Then again, it tends to be seen that it is quick for some web applications as well.

Run-time Errors

The Python language is powerfully composed so it has many structure confinements that are accounted for by some Python engineers. It has been observed that it requires, overall, more testing time, and the blunders show up when the applications are at last run.

Underdeveloped Database Access Layers

When contrasted with innovations like JDBC and ODBC, the Python's database access layer is seen as bit immature and crude. Notwithstanding, it can't be applied in the ventures that need smooth cooperation of complex heritage information.

Installing the Python Interpreter

Before we can compose our initial Python program, we need to download the fitting translator for our PCs.

We'll be utilizing Python 3 in this book on the grounds that as expressed on the official Python site "Python 2.x is inheritance, Python 3.x is the present and fate of the language". What's more, "Python 3 takes out numerous idiosyncrasies that can superfluously entangle starting programmers".

Nonetheless, note that Python 2 is at present still rather broadly utilized. Python 2 and 3 are about 90% comparable. Subsequently on the off chance that you learn Python 3, you will probably have no issues understanding codes written in Python 2.

To introduce the mediator for Python 3, head over to https://www.python.org/downloads/. The correct version ought to be shown at the highest point of the webpage. Snap on the version for Python 3 and the product will begin downloading.

On the other hand in the event that you need to introduce an alternate version, look down the page and you will see a posting of various versions. Snap on the discharge version that you need. We will be utilizing version 3.4.2 in this book. You'll be diverted to the download page for that version.

Look down towards the finish of the page and you'll see a table posting different installers for that version. Pick the correct installer for your PC. The installer to utilize relies upon two variables:

• The working framework (Windows, Mac OS, or Linux) and

• The processor (32-bit versus 64-bit) that you are utilizing.

For example, in the event that you are utilizing a 64-bit Windows PC, you will probably be utilizing the "Windows x86-64 MSI installer". Simply click on the connection to download it. On the off chance that you download and run an inappropriate installer, no stresses. You will get a mistake message and the translator won't introduce. Just download the correct installer and you are a great idea to go.

When you have effectively introduced the mediator, you are prepared to begin coding in Python.

Utilizing the Python Shell, IDLE and Writing our FIRST program

We'll be composing our code utilizing the IDLE program that comes packaged with our Python mediator.

To do that, allows first dispatch the IDLE program. You dispatch the IDLE program like how you dispatch some other programs. For example on Windows 8, you can scan for it by composing "IDLE" in the hunt box. When it is discovered, click on IDLE (Python GUI) to dispatch it. You'll be given the Python Shell demonstrated as follows.

The Python Shell enables us to utilize Python in intuitive mode. This implies we can enter each order in turn. The Shell sits tight for an order from the user, executes it and returns the aftereffect of the execution. After this, the Shell hangs tight for the following direction.

Try by typing the following into the Shell. The lines beginning with >>> are the directions you should type while the lines after the directions demonstrate the outcomes.

```
>>> 2+3
5
>>> 3>2
True
>>> print ('Hello World') Hello World
```

When you type 2+3, you are giving a direction to the Shell, soliciting it to assess the incentive from 2+3. Consequently, the Shell restores the appropriate response 5. When you type 3>2, you are inquiring as to whether 3 is more noteworthy than 2. The Shell answers True. At long last, print is a direction requesting that the Shell show the line Hello World.

The Python Shell is an advantageous instrument for testing Python directions, particularly when we are first beginning with the language. In any event that you exit from the Python Shell and enter it once more, each one of the directions you type will be no more. Also, you cannot utilize the Python Shell to create a genuine program. To code a genuine program, you have to compose your code in a book document and spare it with a .py expansion. This record is known as a Python script.

To make a Python script, click on File > New File in the top menu of our Python Shell. This will raise the word processor that we are going to use to compose our absolute first program, the "Welcome World" program. Composing the "Welcome World" program is somewhat similar to the soul changing experience for every single new software engineer. We'll be utilizing this program to acclimate ourselves with the IDLE programming.

Input the following into the text editor .

#Prints the Words "Hello World" print ("Hi World")

The line #Prints the Words "Hi World" (in red) is not a part of the program but a feedback written to make our code more readable for other programmers and users. This line is overlooked by the Python interpreter and add comments to our program, we type a # sign in front of each line of comment:
You should see that the line #Prints the Words "Hi World" is in red while "print" is in purple and "Hi World" is in green. This is the product's method for making our code simpler to peruse. The words "print" and "Hi World" fill various needs in our program, thus they are shown utilizing various colors.
#This
is
a comment

#This
is
also a comment

In another way, we can decide to use three single quotes (or three double quotes) for a multiline comments, just like this:

,,,

This
is
a comment

This
is
also a comment.

'''

You can now click File > Save As... to store your code. Be sure that you save it with the extension .py.

Are you done? Voilà! You have just successfully written your 1st program in python.

Finally, click on Run > Run Module to run the program or simply press F5. You can now see the words Hello World printed on your Python Shell.

Terms You Should Know with Python

Before you get too so much into your programming with Python, it is critical to see a portion of the words that can make the programming clearer. This section is going to set aside some effort to take a gander at the various words that are basic in Python programming, and which we do discuss a piece in this manual, to help maintain a strategic distance from some perplexity and allows you to begin with your first code.

• Class—this is a format that was utilized for making client characterized objects.

• Docstring—this is a string that will show up lexically first articulation inside a module, capacity, or class definition. The object will be accessible to documentation devices.

• Function—this is a square of code that is summoned when utilizing a calling program. It is best utilized so as to give a figuring or a self-governing help.

• IDLE—this represents Integrated Development Environment for Python. It is an essential mediator and manager condition that you can use alongside Python. It is useful for the individuals who are simply starting with this and can work for those on a spending limit. It is a reasonable case of code and won't burn through a ton of time or space.

• Immutable—this is an object inside the code that is appointed a fixed worth. This could incorporate tuples, strings, and numbers. You can't adjust the object and you should make another object with an alternate worth and store it first. This can be useful sometimes, for example, the keys in a word reference.

• Interactive—one thing that a ton of apprentices like about Python is that it is so intelligent. You can evaluate some various things in the mediator and perceive how they will respond immediately in the outcomes. It is a decent method to improve your programming aptitudes, try out another thought you have and then some.

• List—this is a data type inside Python that is inherent. It contains an impermanent succession of values that are arranged. It can incorporate permanent values of numbers and strings also.

• Mutable—these are the objects that will have the option to change their incentive inside the program, however which can keep their unique id ().

• Object—inside Python, this is any data with a state, for example, a worth or a quality, just as a characterized conduct, or a strategy.

• Python 3000— The Python 2 and Python 3 are the principle two types of Python that are accessible. Numerous individuals have stayed with Python 2 since Python 3 doesn't have any regressive abilities and they like utilizing the databases on the more established form. Python 3000 is a legendary choice of Python that allows this regressive ability so you can utilize it and the Python 2.

• String—this is one of the most fundamental types that you will discover in Python that will store the content. In Python 2, the strings will store message with the goal that the string type would then be able to be utilized to clutch double data.

• Triple cited string—this is a string that has three examples of either the single statement or the twofold statement. It could have something like " I cherish tacos' '. They are utilized for some reasons. They can assist you with having twofold and single statements in a string and they make it simpler to go over a couple of lines of code without issues.

• Tuple—this is a data type that has been incorporated with Python. This data type is a changeless arranged succession of values. The grouping is the main part that is unchanging. It can contain some impermanent values, for example, having a lexicon inside it, where the values can change.

• Type—this is a class or kind of data that is spoken to in the programming dialects. These types will contrast in their properties, they including changeless and variable alternatives, just as in their capacities and strategies. Python incorporates a couple of these including word reference types, tuple, list, coasting point, long, whole number, and string.

Presently the time has come to become more acquainted with more about Python programming and how you can make it work for you. You should gain proficiency with more about the various watchwords and the factors that accompany Python so you can compose the words that you need and make the program perform with a particular goal in mind. We should investigate a portion of these nuts and bolts of Python programming so you can begin with your new code immediately.

Keywords

When you are taking a shot at another PC coding program, you are going to see that every coding languages will have certain catchphrases. These are the words that are intended for a particular direction or reason in the language and you should attempt to abstain from utilizing them anyplace else. In the event that you do utilize these words in different pieces of your code, you may wind up with a blunder alert or the program not working appropriately. The watchwords that are saved for Python include:

· None
· And
· Pass
· Or
· not
· Nonlocal
· Lambda
· Is
· In
· For
· Finally

· False
· Except
· Import
· If
· Global
· From
· Break
· Assert
· Else
· Elif
· Del
· Def
· Continue
· Class
· While
· Try
· True
· Return
· Raise
· As
· Yield
· With

The World of Variables and Operators

Since we're finished with the early on stuff, we should get down to the genuine stuff. Factors and administrators will be talked about in subtleties. In particular, you'll realize what factors mean and how to appropriately name and pronounce them. We'll likewise find out about the regular activities that we can perform on them. Are you game? We should go. Variables refer to the names given to data that we require to store and manipulate in our programs. For example, on the off chance that your program needs to store the age of a client. To achieve that, we should name this data userAge and characterize the variable userAge utilizing the accompanying articulation.

userAge = 0

After defining the variable userAge, your program will allocate a certain portion of your computer's storage space to store this data. Then you can access and modify this data by referring to it by its name, userAge. When you declare a new variable anytime, you need to give it an initial value.

In this example, we assigned to it the value 0. We can also decide to change this value in our program later. Also, we can define multiple variables at one go. To do that simply, write
userAge, userName = 30, 'Paul'
This is equivalent to
userAge = 30 userName = 'Paul'

A variable name in Python can just contain letters (a - z, A - B), numbers or underscores (_). In any condition or case, the main character can't be a number. Thus, you can name your factors userName, user_name or userName2 yet not 2userName.

What's more, there are some reserved words that you can't use as a variable name since they as of now have pre-doled out implications in Python. These saved words incorporate words like print, input, if, while and so forth.
At long last, variable names are case sensitive. username isn't equivalent to userName.
There are two shows when naming a variable in Python. We can either utilize the camel case notation or use underscores. Camel case is the act of composing compound words with mixed casing (for example thisIsAVariableName). This is the show that we'll be utilizing with in the remainder of the book. On the other hand, another basic practice is to utilize underscores (_) to isolate the

words. In the event that you like, you can name your variables like this: this_is_a_variable_name.

Identifier Names

When you are making another program in Python, you are getting down to business on making many substances, a mix of capacities, classes, and factors. All of these will be given a name that is otherwise called an identifier. There are a couple of guidelines that you have to pursue when shaping an identifier in Python including:

It ought to contain letters, either capitalized or lowercase or a blend

of the two, numbers, and the underscore. You ought not perceive any spaces inside.

The identifier can't begin with a number

The identifier can't be a catchphrase and it should exclude one of the watchwords inside.

In the event that you defy one of these norms, the program will close on you and will demonstrate a language structure blunder. Likewise, you have to take a shot at making identifiers that are readable to human. While the identifier might be to the PC and get past without causing issues on the PC, a human is the person who will peruse the code to utilize it themselves. On the off chance that the human eye doesn't comprehend what you are writing in a specific spot, you could keep running into certain issues. A portion of the principles that you ought to pursue when making an identifier that will be meaningful to the human eye include:

The identifier ought to be clear—you should select name that will portray what is inside the variable or will depict what it does.

You ought to be cautious with utilizing condensings that aren't vital in light of the fact that these consistently make things that are troublesome.

While there are a great deal of ways that you can work out your code, you ought to be cautious and stick with one principle all through. For instance, both MyBestFriend and mybestfriend work in the coding scene, yet pick one that you like and do it the equivalent each time that you work in the program to maintain a strategic distance from perplexity. You can likewise include underscores into this or numbers, simply be cautious that you keep things reliable.

Flow of Control

When taking a shot at the Python language, you will work out the anstatements in a rundown position, much the same as you would when working out a shopping list. The PC will begin with the principal guidance before working through every one of them in the request that you make them appear on the rundown. So you should work out the controls that you need simply like you would for your shopping for food rundown to make sure that the PC is perusing it appropriately. The PC will just quit perusing this rundown once it has done the last guidance to finish. This is known as the progression of control.

This is a significant method to begin. You need to make sure that your progression of control is even and smooth for the PC to peruse. This will make it simpler to get the program to do what you might want without the same number of issues and guarantees that the PC program doesn't stall out, cause issues, or have something different turn out badly.

Semi-colons and Indentation

When you take a gander at a portion of the other programming languages, you will see that there are a great deal of wavy sections used to orchestrate the various squares of code or to start and end the announcements. This causes you to make sure to indent the code obstructs in these dialects to make the code simpler to peruse, despite the fact that the PC will have the option to peruse the various codes without the spaces fine and dandy.

This type of coding can make it extremely hard to peruse. You will see a ton of superfluous data that is required for the PC to peruse the code, yet can make it hard on the human eye to understand this. Python utilizes an alternate method for doing this, generally to help make it simpler on the human eye to peruse what you have. You are going to need to indent the code for this to work. A case of this is:

 # this function definition starts another square

def add_numbers (b, c): d= b + c
as is this one

return **d**

 # this function definition is the start of a new-block

if it is Snday

print (It's Wednesday!"

 # and this particular one is outside of this block

print ("Print this no matter what.")

In addition, there exist a lot of languages that will use a semicolon to indicate when an instruction ends.
In any case, Python however, you will utilize line finishes to tell the PC when a guidance will end. You'll have the option to utilize a

semi-colon on the off chance that you have a couple of guidelines that are on a similar line, yet this is frequently viewed as inappropriate behavior inside the language.

Letter Case

Most scripts will treat capitalized and lowercase letters the equivalent, however Python is one of the main ones that will be case touchy. This implies the lower case and capitalized letters will be dealt with distinctively in the framework. Remember too that all the saved words will utilize lower case aside from None, False, and genuine.

These rudiments are going to make it simpler to begin on the Python programming. You have to set aside a touch of effort to experience the program so as to get acquainted with it. You won't have to turn into a specialist, however getting acquainted with a portion of the content mediator and a portion of different pieces of the program can make it simpler to utilize and you can figure out how the various catches will function even before you begin. Evaluate a couple of the models above first to enable you to begin.

Python attempts to keep things as essential as conceivable on the grounds that it comprehends that the greater part of its clients will be learners or the individuals who are sick of other complex dialects. As should be obvious here, and in the accompanying sections, there are straightforward directions that you will have the option to take care of forward to get the program to work a particular way. Concentrate these and you can make an incredible program without very as much work.

Remarks/comments in Python

There are a great deal of things that you can do in Python. It is one of the most intelligent alternatives that you will keep running into when beginning in programming and since it is so natural to utilize. In this part, we will set aside some effort to examine progressively about remarks and a portion of different parts of Python so you can begin and make your codes astonishing in a matter of seconds.

In Python programming a remark is one that will begin with the # sign and after that will proceed until you get as far as possible of the line. For instance:

 # There are going be just another comments

print("Hello, How are you doing?)

This would advise the PC to simply print "Hello, how are you doing?" All remarks are disregarded in the Python mediator since it is to a greater degree a commentary in the program to support the software engineer, or other people who may utilize the code, extraordinary things about the code. They are essentially there to state what the program should do and how it will function. It is more itemized and can be useful without hindering how the code functions.

You won't have to leave a remark on each line, exactly when it is required. In the event that the software engineer feels that something needs clarified better, they would place in a remark yet don't hope to see it everywhere. Python doesn't bolster any remarks that will go over a few lines so on the off chance that you have a more drawn out remark in the program, make sense of how to separate it into various lines with the # sign before each part.

Composing and Reading

A couple of projects will show the substance you need on the screen, or they can request certain data. You may need to start the program code by telling the peruser what your program is about.

Assigning it a name or a title can make things less complex so the other coder grasps what is in the program and can pick the correct one for them.

The most ideal approach to get the correct data to show up is demonstrate a string strict that will incorporate the "print" work. For the individuals who don't have the foggiest idea, string literals are essentially lines of content that will be encompassed by certain statements, either a solitary or twofold statement. The type of statement that you use won't make any difference that much, yet on the off chance that you utilize one type in the start of the expression, you should utilize it toward the end. So if there are twofold statements toward the start of your expression, make sure that you stay aware of the twofold statements toward the end too.

When you need the PC to show a word or expression on the screen, you would essentially have "print" and afterward the expression after it. For instance, in the event that you need to depict.

 "Hi, welcome!" you would do
Print("Welcome!")

This will make it so that "Welcome" pop up on your program for others to use. The print function will take up its very own line so you will see that in the wake of placing this in, the code will consequently put you on another line.
Probably you might want to have the guest do a specific activity, you can go with a similar sort of thought. For instance, say you need the individual to enter a particular number with the goal that they can traverse the code you would utilize the string:

second_number = input('put the second number in.')

When utilizing the input feature, you won't consequently observe it print on another line. The content will be set just after the brief. You will likewise need to change over the string into a number for the program to work. You don't have to have a particular parameter for this either. On the off chance that you do the accompanying alternative with simply the enclosures and nothing inside, you will get a similar outcome and in some cases makes it simpler.

Chapter 2: Files

Generally, you will utilize the print capacity to get a string to print to the screen. This is the default of the print work, however you can likewise utilize this equivalent capacity as a decent method to compose something onto a document. A genuine case of this is here: with open('myfile.txt', 'v) as myfile: Print("Hello there!",file=myfile)

Presently this may resemble a basic condition, however there is a lot that is going on in the string over that you should watch out for. At the point when you opened up the myfile.txt to compose on and after that doled out it to the variable called myfile. At that point in the subsequent part, you wrote in Hello! To the record as another line and after that the w told the program that you may have the option to compose the progressions when the document is open.

Obviously, you don't need to utilize the print capacity to get it to take every necessary step that you need. The compose technique will frequently function admirably as well. For instance, you can supplant the print with compose like the model beneath to get very similar things.

with open('myfile.txt', 'v') as myfile: myfile.write("Hello there!")

So far, we have figured out how to print a string of words into the program and even how to spare them to a particular record. Notwithstanding those alternatives, you can utilize the read technique so as to open a particular document and afterward to peruse the data that is there. If perhaps that you might want to open and peruse a particular record, utilize this choice:

With open('myfile.txt', 'w') as my file:
data = my file. read ()

With this option, the program will be instructed to read up the files contents to a variable data. This can make it much easier to open up those programs that you might love to read later.

Built In Types

Your PC is equipped for handling a great deal of data including numbers and characters. The types of data that the Python program will utilize are known as types and the language will contain a wide range of types to help make things simpler. A portion of these incorporate string, whole numbers, and coasting point numbers. Software engineers can even characterize these various types utilizing classes.

Types will comprise of two separate parts. The initial segment is an area that will contain a conceivable arrangement of values and the subsequent part is a set that contains the potential activities. Both of these can be carried out on any worth. A case of this is on the off chance that you have a space that is a type of number; it can just contain whole numbers inside it including expansion, division, duplication, and subtraction.

One thing to note with this is Python is a progressively typed program. This implies there truly isn't a need to determine the types for the factors when you make it. Similar factors can be utilized to store the values of various types. Regardless of this, Python still needs you to have every one of the factors with a complete type. For instance, if the software engineer attempted to include a number to a string, the Python program would perceive this and demonstrate a mistake. It won't attempt to make sense of what you needed; rather it will simply exit easily.

Integers

If you need to utilize integers as a type, you have to keep them as entire numbers. These can be certain or negative numbers, insofar as there are no decimals with these numbers. In the event that you have a decimal point in the number, regardless of whether the number is 1.0, you should utilize it as a coasting point number.

Python can show these whole numbers in the "print" work, however just on the off chance that it is the sole contention.
Print(3)
# Let's include two numbers together
Print(1+2)

Also, if that you are utilizing whole numbers, you won't have the option to put the two appropriate beside one another. This is mostly a result of how Python is a specifically language and won't remember them on the off chance that you join them together. Youmight want to put the number and the string together, you have to make sure that the number has transformed to string.

Operator Precedence

One thing that you have to monitor when you are working in Python is administrator priority. For instance, on the off chance that you have 1+2//3 Python could translate it as (1+2)//3 or 1+(2//3). Python has a strategy that will assist you with ordering the activity appropriately so you get the correct data to come up. For instance, with regards to whole number activity, Python is going to deal with everything that is sections first. At that point it will deal with the things that have**, at that point

*, and afterward/, then %, +, lastly - .

In the event that you are composing an articulation that has various tasks in it, you should remember those signs. This will disclose to Python how to experience the numbers with the goal that you can get the correct answers at the time. Remember that most number juggling administrators will be left acquainted so work it out that path for Python to peruse. The main special case is the ** include. For instance:

** is correct acquainted 2**3**4
will be assessed appropriate to left:
2**(3**4)

Strings

While a string may appear to be something confounded, in Python they are essentially a grouping of characters. They are getting down to business a similar path as a rundown does, yet they will contain more usefulness that is explicit to the content.

Designing strings can be a test with regards to working out your out your code. There are a few messages that won't be fixed string and once in a while there are values that are stored inside factors inside it. There is an approach to get this to work directly for string arranging. A case of this is:

Name = "Janet" Age = 24

Print("Hello! My name is %s." % name)

The images that have a % first are called placeholders. The factors that go into these positions will be set after the % in the request where they are put in the string. On the off chance that you are doing only a solitary string, you won't require a wrapper, yet on the off chance that you do have more than one of these, you have to put them into a tuple, with a () walling it in. The placeholder images will begin with various letters, depending for the most part on the variable type you are utilizing. For instance, the age will be a whole number by the name is a string. These factors will be changed over into the string before you can include them into the rest.

Escape Sequences

The escape sequence can be utilized as an approach to mean uncommon characters that can be difficult to type on your console. Moreover, they can be utilized to indicate characters that can be held for something different. For instance, utilizing and in the arrangement can befuddle the program so you may utilize the departure succession to supplant that like the accompanying model:

Print("This is a line. \nThis is a different line.")

Triple Quotes

We have invested a touch of energy discussing both single and twofold statements, however there are times when you may need to get the triple statement. This is utilized when you have to characterize an exacting that will traverse numerous lines or one that as of now has a great deal of statements in it. To do this, simply utilize a solitary and twofold together or three singles. A similar standard applies with the triple statement likewise with all the others. You should begin and close the expression with the equivalent trile quote.

Chapter 3: String Operations

One of the string tasks that you may utilize a great deal is a connection. This is utilized so as to join a couple of strings together and you will see it is there with the + image. There are a great deal of capacities that Python can assist you with and they will work with the strings to make an assortment of tasks. They will have some valuable choices that can do much more in the Pythons program

In Python program, strings are called changeless. This implies once you make the string, it isn't fit for being changed. You may need to dole out another important to a particular variable that exists on the off chance that you are hoping to make a few changes.

There is so much that you are able to learn about when it comes to getting started with Python. It may be a simple language, but you want to be able to learn how it works, how to write things down properly, and even how to leave a comment for others to understand when they are looking through the code. It may seem a bit intimidating in the beginning, but before too long, and with some practice, you will get it down and be writing your own code in no time.

The Assignment Sign

Take note that the = sign in the statement userAge = 0 has quite a number of meaning from the = sign we learned in Math. In python programming, the = sign is known as an assignment sign. It connotes that we are assigning the value which is on the right side of the = sign to the variable on the left. A great method to understand the statement userAge = 0 is to have the thought of it as the userAge <- 0.

The statements y = z and z = y . have very different meanings in programming

Confused? An example will likely clear this up.

Input the following code into your IDLE editor and save it up.

```
y = 5
z = 10
y = z
print ("y = ", y)
print ("z = ", z)
```

Now run the program. You should get this output:

```
y = 10
z = 10
```

Although our x has an initial value of 5 (declared on the first line), the third line y = z assigns the value of z to y (y <- z), hence changing the value of y to 10 while the value of z is still unchanged.

Next up, modify the program by changing ONLY ONE statement: Change the third line from y = z to z = y. Mathematically, y = z and z = y mean the same thing. However, this is not so when it comes to programming.

Run the second program. You will now get

```
y = 10
z = 10
```

You can notice that in this example, the y value remains as 10, but the value of z is changed to 10. This is because the statement z = y assigns the value of y to z (z <- y). z becomes 10 while y remains unchanged as 10.

Basic Operators

Other than relegating a variable an underlying value, we can likewise play out the standard scientific activities on factors. Essential administrators in Python incorporate +, - ,/, % and * which speak to expansion, subtraction, augmentation, division, floor division, modulus and exponent separately.

Example:

Suppose y = 10, z = 4 Addition: y + z = 7 Subtraction: y - z = 3
Multiplication: y*z = 10 Division: y/z = 4.10
Floor Division: y//z = 4 (rounds down the answer to the nearest whole number)
Modulus: y%z = 1 (gives the remainder when 10 is divided by 4)
Exponent: y**z = 410 (10 to the power of 4)

More on Assignment Operators.

In addition to the = sign, there are a few more assignment operators in Python (and other programming languages). These include operators like +=, -= and *=.

Suppose we have the variable y, with an initial value of 10. If we want to increment y bz 4, we can write
y = y + 4

The program will first evaluate the eypression on the right (y + 4) and assign the answer to the left. So eventuallz the statement above becomes y <- 14.

Instead of writing y = y + 4, we can also write y += 4 to express the same meaning. The += sign is actually a shorthand that adds the assignment sign with the addition operator. Hence, y += 4 simply means y = y + 4.

39

Similarly, if we would love to do a subtraction, we can write y = y - 4 or y - = 4. The same thing works for all the 7 operators mentioned in the section above.

Chapter 4: Data Types in Python

In this chapter, we'll take a critical look at some basic data types in Python, categorically the integer, float and string. Moving forward, we'll explore the concept of type casting. Lastly, we'll talk about three more advanced data types in Python which are the list, tuple and dictionary.

Integers

Integers are those numbers without decimal parts, such as -6, -5, -2, 0, 2, 6 etc.

To declare an integer in Python programming, simply write variableName = initial value

Example:
userAge = 50, mobileNumber = 12398724

Float

Float is the name given to numbers that have decimal parts, such as 1.234, -0.023, 12.01.

To declare a float in Python, we will write variableName = initial value

Example:
userHeight. = 2.92, userWeight = 67.5

String

String also refers to text.

To declare a string, you might either utilize variableName = 'initial value' (single quotes) or variableName = "initial value" (double quotes)

Example:
userName = 'Peter', userSpouseName = "Janet", userAge = '30'

In retrospect to our last example, because we used userAge = '30', userAge is a string. Otherwise, if you typed userAge = 30 (without quotes), userAge is known as the integer.

You can also combine different substrings by using the concatenate sign (+). For example, "Paul" + "Lee" is equivalent to the string "PaulLee".

Built-In String Functions

Python has many of built-in functions which are used to manipulate strings. A function is basically a block of reusable code that performs a certain task.

A good example of a function available in Python is the upper() method for strings. You use it for capitalizing all the letters in a string. For example, 'Paul'.upper() will give us the string "PAUL".

Type Casting In Python

Sometimes in python program, it is necessary for us to convert from one data type to another, such as from an integer to a string. This is known as type casting.

There are essentially 3 built in function in Python that enable us to perform type casting in python programming. These include the int(), float(), and str() functions.

The int() work in Python takes in a buoy or a proper string and changes over it to a number. To change over a buoy to a whole number, we can type int(5.712987). We'll have 5 as the outcome (anything after the decimal point is evacuated). To change a string to a whole number, we can type int ("4") and we'll get 4. Nonetheless, we can't type int ("Hello") or int ("4.22321"). We'll get a blunder in the two cases.

The buoy() work takes in a whole number or a suitable string and changes it to a buoy. For example, on the off chance that we type float(2) or float("2"), we'll get 2.0. In the event that we type float("2.09109"), we'll get 2.09109 which is a buoy and not a string since the quotes are expelled.

The str() work then again changes over a whole number or a buoy to a string. For example, on the off chance that we type str(2.1), we'll get "2.1".

Since we've secured the three essential data types in Python and their throwing, we should proceed onward to the further developed data types.

List

List alludes to an accumulation of data which are typically related. Rather than putting away these data as discrete factors, we can store them as a rundown. For example, assume our program needs to store the age of 5 clients. Rather than putting away them as user1Age, user2Age, user3Age, user4Age and user5Age, it makes more sense to store them as a rundown.

To pronounce a list, you compose listName = [initial values]. Note that we utilize square sections [ ] when proclaiming a rundown. Various values are isolated by a comma.

Model:

userAge = [21, 22, 23, 24, 25]

We can likewise pronounce a list/rundown without appointing any underlying values to it. We essentially compose listName = []. What we have now is an unfilled rundown without any things in it. We need to utilize the attach() strategy referenced beneath to add things to the rundown.

Individual values in the rundown are open by their lists, and records consistently start from ZERO, not 1. This is a typical practice in practically all programming dialects, for example, C and Java. Subsequently the primary worth has a list of 0, the following has a file of 1, etc. For example, userAge[0] = 21, userAge[1] = 22

On the other hand, you can get to the values of a rundown from the back. The last thing in the rundown has a record of - 1, the subsequent last has a file of - 2, etc. Subsequently, userAge[-1] = 25, userAge[-2] = 24.

You can allocate a rundown, or some portion of it, to a variable. On the off chance that you compose userAge2 = userAge, the variable userAge2 progresses toward becoming [21, 22, 23, 24, 25].

In the event that you compose userAge3 = userAge[2:4], you are relegating things with list 2 to list 4-1 from the rundown userAge to the rundown userAge3. As it were, userAge3 = [23, 24].

The documentation 2:4 is known as a cut. At whatever point we utilize the cut documentation in Python, the thing toward the beginning list is constantly included, however the thing toward the

44

end is constantly prohibited. Henceforth the documentation 2:4 alludes to things from list 2 to list 4-1 (for example file 3), which is the reason userAge3 = [23, 24] and not [23, 24, 25].

The cut documentation incorporates a third number known as the stepper. On the off chance that we compose userAge4 = userAge[1:5:2], we will get a sub rundown comprising of consistently number from file 1 to file 5-1 in light of the fact that the stepper is 2. Thus, userAge4 = [22, 24].

Furthermore, cut documentations have helpful defaults. The default for the primary number is zero, and the default for the subsequent number is size of the rundown being cut. For example, userAge[:4] gives you esteems from file 0 to file 4-1 while userAge[1:] gives you esteems from list 1 to file 5-1 (since the size of userAge is 5, for example userAge has 5 things).

To change things in a rundown, we compose listName[index of thing to be modified] = new worth. For example, on the off chance that you need to adjust the subsequent thing, you compose userAge[1] = 5. Your rundown progresses toward becoming userAge = [21, 5, 23, 24, 25]

To include things, you utilize the attach() work. For example, in the event that you use userAge.append(99), you add the worth 99 as far as possible of the rundown. Your rundown is presently userAge = [21, 5, 23, 24, 25, 99]

To expel things, you compose del listName[index of thing to be deleted]. For example, in the event that you use del userAge[2], your rundown presently progresses toward becoming userAge = [21, 5, 24, 25, 99] (the third thing is erased).
To fully appreciate the usefulness of lists, run the following code.

# list elements can include different types:
myList = [1, 2, 3, 4, 5, "Hello"]

45

```python
#print the whole list.
print(myList)

#You'll have [1, 2, 3, 4, 5, "Hello"]

#print the third object(remember: Indexes start at zero).
print(myList[2])
#It will print 3

#print the last item.
print(myList[-1])
#It will print "Hello"

#assign myList (index 1 to 4) to myList2, then print myList2
myList2 = myList[1:4]
print (myList2)
#It will print [2, 3, 4, 5]

#edit the 2nd item in myList, then print the updated list
myList[1] = 20
print(myList)
#It will print [1, 20, 3, 4, 5, 'Hello']

#append a new string to myList and print the new list

myList.append("How are you")
print(myList)

#It will print [1, 20, 3, 4, 5, 'Hello', 'How are you']


#delete the 6th item from myList, then print the list
del
myList[5]
print(myList)
```

#It will print [1, 20, 3, 4, 5, 'How are you']

Tuple

Tuples are much the same as lists, however you can't alter their qualities. The underlying qualities are the qualities that will remain for the remainder of the program. A Dictionary where tuples are helpful is the point at which your program has to cache the names of the months of the year.

To pronounce a tuple, you compose tupleName = (starting qualities). Notice that we use round sections ( ) when announcing a tuple. Numerous qualities are isolated by a comma.

Dictionary:

monthsOfYear = ("Jan", "Feb", "March", "Apr", "May",
"Jun", "Jul", "Aug", "Sep", "Oct", "Nov", "Dec")

You get to the individual estimations of a tuple utilizing their records, much the same as with a list.

Subsequently, monthsOfYear[0] = "Jan", monthsOfYear[-1] = "Dec".

Dictionary

Dictionary is an accumulation of related information PAIRS. For example, in the event that we need to store the username and age of 5 clients, we can store them in a dictionary.

To proclaim a dictionary, you compose dictionaryName = {dictionary key : data}, with the necessity that dictionary keys must be special (inside one dictionary). Along these lines, it is beyond the realm of imagination to expect to proclaim a dictionary like this myDictionary = {"Peter":38, "John":51, "Peter":13}.

The explanation is that "Subside" is utilized as the dictionary key twice. Note that we utilize wavy sections { } when announcing a dictionary. Various sets are isolated by a comma.

Dictionary:

userNameAndAge = {"Paul":38, "John":51, "Alley":13, "Alvin":"Not Available"}

You can likewise proclaim a dictionary utilizing the dict( ) strategy. To announce the userNameAndAge dictionary above, you compose userNameAndAge = dict(Paul= 38, John = 51, Alley = 13, Alvin = "Not Available")

When you utilisize this strategy to proclaim a dictionary, you utilize round sections ( ) rather than wavy sections { } and you don't put quotes for the dictionary keys.

To arrive at the individual things in the dictionary, we utilize the dictionary key, which is the primary incentive in the {dictionary key : data} pair. For example, to get John's age, you input userNameAndAge["John"].

You'll get the worth 51.

To change things in a dictionary, we compose dictionaryName[dictionary key of thing to be modified] = new information.

For example, to change the "John":51 pair, we compose userNameAndAge["John"] = 21. Our dictionary presently progresses toward becoming userNameAndAge = {"Paul":38, "John":21, "Alley":13, "Alvin":"Not Available"}.

It is additionally conceivable to announce a dictionary without doling out any underlying qualities to it. We basically compose dictionaryName = { }. What we have now is an unfilled dictionary without any things in it.

To add things to a dictionary, we compose dictionaryName[dictionary key] = information. For example, on the off chance that we need to include "Joe":40 to our dictionary, we compose userNameAndAge["Joe"] = 40. Our dictionary presently progresses toward becoming userNameAndAge = {"Peter":38, "John":21, "Alex":13, "Alvin":"Not Available", "Joe":40}

To expel things from a dictionary, we compose del dictionaryName[dictionary key]. For example, to expel the "Alex":13 pair, we compose del userNameAndAge["Alley"]. Our dictionary currently moves toward becoming userNameAndAge = {"Peter":38, "John":21, "Alvin":"Not Available", "Joe":40}

Run the accompanying system to see all these in real life.

#declaring the dictionary, dictionary keys and information can be of various information kinds

myDict = {"One":1.35, 4.5:"Two Point Five", 3:"+", 7.9:3}

#print the whole dictionary.

print(myDict)

#You'll get {4.5: 'Two Point Five', 3: '+', 'One': 1.35, 7.9: 3}

#Note the fact that things in a dictionary are not put away in a similar request as the manner in which you announce them.

#print the thing with key = "One". print(myDict["One"])

#You'll get 1.35

#print the thing with key = 7.9. print(myDict[7.9])

#You'll get 2

#modify the thing with key = 2.5 and print the refreshed dictionary

myDict[2.5] = "Over two" print(myDict)

#You'll get {2.5: 'Over two', 3: '+', 'One': 1.35, 7.9: 2}

#add another thing and print the refreshed dictionary myDict["New item"] = "I'm new"

print(myDict)

#You'll get {'New thing': 'I'm new', 2.5: 'Over two', 3: '+', 'One': 1.35, 7.9: 2}

#remove the thing with key = "One" and print the refreshed dictionary

```
del myDict["One"]
print(myDict)
```

Chapter 5: Making Python Programming More Interactive

Since we've secured the fundamentals of variables, let us compose a program that utilizes them. We'll return to the "Welcome World" program prior yet this time we'll make it intuitive. Rather than trying to say hi to the world, we need the world to know our names and ages as well. So as to do that, our program should have the option to provoke us for data and show them on the screen.

Two inherent capacities can do that for us: information() and print(). For the time being, how about we type the accompanying project in IDLE. Spare it and run it.

myName = input("Please input your Name: ")
myAge = input("Please enter your age also: ")

You will print (hi Every one, my name is, myName, "and I am", myAge, "years old.")

The program should incite you for your name.

If it's not too much stress enter your name:

Assumed you entered James. Presently press Enter and it'll incite you for your age.

Shouldn't something be said about your age:

Let's assume you entered in 20. Presently press Enter once more. You ought to get the accompanying proclamation:

Hi World, my name is James and I am 20 years of age.
Input ()
In the model above, we used the input() work twice to get the user's name and age.
myName = input("Kindly input your first name: ")
The string "Please enter your first name: " is the concise that will be showed up on the screen to hand-off rules to the customer. After the customer enters the significant information, this information is taken care of as a string in the variable myName. The accompanying input clarification prompts the customer for his age and stores the information as a string in the variable myAge.
The input() work shifts hardly in Python 2 and Python 3. In Python 2, if you have to recognize customer input as a string, you have to use the raw_input() work.

Print()

The print() work is used to demonstrate information to customers. It recognizes at any rate zero explanations as parameters, disengaged by commas.

In the declaration underneath, we passed 5 parameters to the print() work. Okay have the option to remember them?

print ("Hi Everyone, my name is", myName, "and I am", myAge, "years old.")

The first is the string "Greetings World, my name is" Coming up next is the variable myName declared using the input limit previously. Sought after is the string "and I am", trailed by the variable myAge finally the string "years old.".

Note that we don't use cites when insinuating the elements myName and myAge. If you use cites, you'll get the yield

Hi Everyone, my name is myName and I am myAge years old.

Or maybe, which is plainly not what we need.

Another way to deal with print a declaration with variables is to use the % formatter. To achieve a comparative yield as the chief print clarification above, we can create

print ("Hi World". Your name is #s and you are years old #s (my name, my age))

By then, to print a comparable clarification going by the association() technique, we form

print ("Hi Everyone, my name is {} and I am {} years old".format(my name, myage))

The print() work is another limit that differentiations in Python 2 and Python 3. You form it without segments in Python 2, like this:

print 'Hello World', my name is " + myName + " and I am " + myAge + " years old"

Triple Quotes

In case you need to demonstrate a long message, you can use the triple-quote picture ('" or """) to navigate your message over various lines. For instance, print ('"Hello World.

My name is Fabian and I am 15 years old."') will give you

Greetings World.

My name is Fabian and I am 15 years old.

This fabricates the weightiness of your text.

Escape Chars

Sometimes we may need to print some specific chars like a tab or a newline.
In this case, you need to use the \ (backslash) character to escape characters that
will, otherwise, have a different meaning.

For example to print a tab, we have to input the backslash character before the
letter t, like this: \t. Without the addition of \ character, the letter t will be printed.
With it, a tab is printed.
Henceforth, on the off chance that you type print ('Hello\tWorld'), you'll get Hello
World

Other generally discovered employments of the oblique punctuation line character
are demonstrated as follows.

>>> demonstrates the direction and the accompanying lines demonstrate the
yield.

\n (Prints a newline)

>>> print ('Hello\nWorld') Hello

World

\\ (Prints the oblique punctuation line character itself)

>>> print ('\\')

\' (Prints twofold statement, so that that the twofold statement doesn't suggest the
finish of the string)
>>> print ('I am 4'8\" tall") I am 4'8"

\' (Print single quote, in such a way that the single quote does not indicate the end
of the string)

>>> print ('I am 4\'8" tall') I am 4'8" tall

In the event that you don't need characters gone before by the \ character to be translated as exceptional characters, you can utilize crude strings by including a r before the primary statement. For instance, on if perhaps that you don't need \t to be translated as a tab, you should type print (r'Hello\tWorld'). You will get Hello\tWorld as the result.

Chapter 6: Making Choices

Congratulations, this is likely the most interesting chapter.
I hope you've liked the course so far. Now, ian this chapter, we'll understand how to make your software smarter, capable of making decisions.
Specifically, we'll be learning the if statement, the for loop and the while loop. These are known as control flow tools because they control the flow. In addition, we'll also take a look at the try & except statements that defines what the program should do in case an error occurs.

Anyway, before we dig into these tools, we have to learn condition statements.

Conditional Statements

Any control flow code involves evaluating a condition statement and behaving accordingly. The software will proceed depending on whether the condition is met or not.

The most common statement is the comparison statement.
If we want to check if two variables have the same value, we use the == sign (double =). For example, if your statement is x == y, you are asking the code to check if the value of x equals the value of y. If they are the same, the condition is met, then the statement will be true. Otherwise, the command will evaluate to false.

Other comparison symbols include != (not equals), < (smaller than), > (greater than), <= (smaller than or equals to) and >= (bigger than or equals to). The list below shows how these symbols can be used and gives examples of statements that will evaluate to True.

Not equals: 5 != 2

Greater than: 5>2

Smaller than: 2<5

Greater than or equals to: 5>=2 5>=5

Smaller than or equals to: 2 <= 5. 2 <= 2

We additionally have three logical operators, and, or, not excessively are helpful in the event that we need to consolidate numerous conditions.

The and administrator/operator returns True if all conditions are met. Else it will return False. For example, the announcement 5==5 and 2>1 will return True since the two conditions are True.

The or administrator will return True if at any rate 1 condition is met. Else it will return False. The announcement 5 > 2 or 7 > 10 or 3 == 2 will return True since the main condition 5>2 is True.

Here, the not operator returns True when the condition immediately after the not keyword is false. Else it will return False. Not 2>5 statement will return True since 2 is not greater than 5.

If Statement

The if statement is known to be one of the most broadly utilized control stream statements. It enables the program to assess if a specific condition is met, and to play out the proper activity dependent on the consequence of the assessment. The sythesis of an if statement is as per the following:

if condition 1 is met: do An elif condition 2 is met: do B elif condition 3 is met: do C elif condition 4 is met: do D else:

do E

elif means "else if" and you can have the same number of elif statements as you like.

If you've coded in different dialects like C or Java previously, you might be amazed to see that no enclosures ( ) are required in Python after the if, elif and else watchword. What's more, Python doesn't use wavy { } sections to characterize the start and end of the if statement. Or maybe, Python utilizes space. Anything indented is treated as a square of code that will be executed if the condition assesses to genuine.

To completely see how the if statement functions, fire up IDLE and key in the accompanying code.

userInput = input('Enter 1 or 2: ')

```
if userInput == "1": print ("Hello World,")

print ("How are you?")

elif userInput == "2": print ("Python Rocks!")

print ("I adore Python") else:

print ("You didn't enter a legitimate number")
```

The program first prompts the client for an info utilizing the information work. The outcome is put away in the userInput variable as a string.

Next the statement if userInput == "1": contrasts the userInput variable and the string "1". If the worth put away in userInput is "1", the program will execute all statements that are indented until the space closes. In this model, it'll print "Hi World", at that point it will be pursued "How are you?"

On the other hand, if the worth put away in userInput is "2", the program will print "Python is Cool", trailed by "I adore Python".

For every single other worth, the program will print "You didn't enter a substantial number".

Run the program multiple times, enter 1, 2 and 3 individually for each run. You'll get the ouput below:

Enter 1 or 2:1 Hello World!, how are you?

Enter 1 or 2: 2 Python is Cool!I adore Python
Enter 1 or 2: 3
You didn't enter a valid number

Inline If

The inline if statement is a less complex type of an if statement and is increasingly helpful if you just need to play out a straightforward undertaking. The linguistic structure is:

Perform Task An if condition is genuine else do Task B

For example,

num1 = 12 if myInt==10 else 13

This statement allots 12 to num1 (Task An) if myInt equivalents to 10. Else it doles out 13 to num1 (Task B).

Another model is

print ("This is task An" if myInt == 10 else "This is task B")

This statement gives "This is task A" (Task An) if myInt equivalents to 10. Else it shows "This is task B" (Task B).

For Loop

Next, let us discuss the for loop. The for loop executes a square of code over and over until the condition in the for explanation is never again substantial.
Looping through an iterable
In Python, an iterable is known to be whatever can be looped over, for example, a string, list or tuple. The linguistic structure for looping through an iterable is as per the following:
for an in iterable: print (a)
Model:
pets = ['cats', 'hounds', 'bunnies', 'hamsters'] for myPets in pets:
print (myPets)
In the program above, we initially announce the rundown pets and give it the individuals 'felines', 'hounds', 'hares' and 'hamsters'. Next the announcement for myPets in pets: loops through the pets list and appoints every part in the rundown to the variable myPets.
The first run through the program goes through the for loop, it doles out 'felines' to the variable myPets. The announcement print (myPets) at that point prints the worth 'felines'. The second time the projects loops through the for articulation, it puts the worth 'hounds' to myPets and prints the worth 'hounds'. The program keeps looping through the rundown until the finish of the rundown is come to.
In the event that you run the program, you'll get
felines
hounds
bunnies hamsters
We can likewise show the list of the individuals in the rundown. To do that, we utilize the list() work.

for record, myPets in enumerate(pets): print (file, myPets)
This will give us the yield
0 cats
1 dogs
2 rabbits
3 hamster

The following model tells the best way to loop through a string.
message = 'Hi'
for I in message: print (I)
The ouput we have :
H
e
l
l
o
Looping through an arrangement of numbers

To loop through an arrangement of numbers, the inherent range() work proves to be useful. The range() work creates a rundown of numbers and has the language structure extend (start, end, step).

In the event that start isn't given, the numbers created will begin from zero.

Note: A helpful hint to recollect here is that in Python (and most programming dialects), except if generally expressed, we generally start from zero.

For example, the file of a rundown and a tuple begins from zero. When utilizing the format() technique for strings, the places of parameters start from zero.

When utilizing the range() work, if start isn't given, the numbers produced start from zero.

On the off chance that progression isn't given, a rundown of back to back numbers will be created (for example step = 1). The end worth must be given. In any case, one strange thing about the range() work is that the given end worth is never part of the produced rundown.

For example,

range(5) will create the rundown [0, 1, 2, 3, 4]

range(3, 10) will create [3, 4, 5, 6, 7, 8, 9]

range(4, 10, 2) will create [4, 6, 8]

To perceive how the range() work works in a for articulation, take a stab at running the accompanying line of code:

for i in range(5): print (i)

You should get
0
1
2
3
4

While Loop

The following control stream statement we are going to take a gander at is the while loop. Like the name recommends, a while loop over and again executes guidelines inside the loop while a specific condition stays legitimate. The syntax of this statement is the following:

while condition is valid: do A

More often than not when utilizing a while loop, we have to initially proclaim a variable to work as a loop counter. Allows simply call this variable counter. The condition in the while statement will assess the estimation of counter to decide whether it littler (or more prominent) than a specific worth. On the off chance that it is, the loop will be executed. How about we take a gander at an example program.
counter = 6

while counter > 1:
print ('Counter' = 'counter') counter = counter -1

If you run the program, you'll get the following output
    Counter
    =

6

Counter
=
5

Counter
=
4

Counter
=
3

Counter
=
2

From the start look, a while statement appears to have the least difficult sentence structure and ought to be the most straightforward to utilize. Notwithstanding, one must be cautious when utilizing while loops because of the threat of limitless loops. In the program above notice that we have the line counter = counter - 1? This line is vital. It diminishes the estimation of counter by 1 and doles out this new incentive back to counter, overwriting the first worth.

We need to bring down the estimation of counter by 1 with the goal that the loop condition while counter > 0 will at long last assess to False. In the event that we forget to do that, the loop will continue running unendingly bringing about a vast loop. In the event that you need to encounter this direct, simply erase the line counter = counter - 1 and have a go at running the program once more. Counter = 5 will continue printing by the program until you by one way or another slaughter the program. This is certainly not a decent encounter particularly on the off chance that you have an enormous program and you have no clue which code portion is causing the boundless loop.

Break

When working with loops, once in a while you might need to leave the whole loop when a specific condition is met. To do that, we utilize the break catchphrase.

Run the accompanying project to perceive how it functions.

j = 0

for I in range(5): j = j + 2

print ('I = ', I, ', j = ', j) if j == 6: break

We ought to get the accompanying yield.

i
=
0

,
j
=
2

i
=
1

,
j
=
4

i
=
2

,
j
=
6

Without the break keyword, the program ideally loops from i = 0 to i = 4 owing to the fact that we used the function range(5). However with the addition of the break keyword, the program closes rashly at I = 2. This is on the grounds that when I = 2, j arrives at the estimation of 6 and the break catchphrase makes the loop end.

In the model above, observe that we used an if statement inside a for loop. It is very expected of us to 'blend and-match' different control devices in programming, for example, utilizing a while loop inside an if statement or utilizing a for loop inside a while loop. This is known as a nested control statement.

Try, Except

The last control statement we'll investigate in this book is the attempt, with the exception of statement. This statement controls how the program continues when a blunder happens. The sentence structure is as per the following:

attempt:

accomplish something with the exception of:

accomplish something different when a blunder happens

For example, take a stab at running the program beneath

attempt:

answer =12/0 print (answer)

but:

print ("A blunder happened")

When you execute the program, you will ll see the message "A blunder happened". This is on the grounds that when the program attempts to execute the statement answer =12/0 in the attempt hinder, a mistake happens since you can't separate a number by zero. The staying of the attempt square is disregarded and the statement in the aside from square is executed.

On the off chance that you need to show progressively explicit mistake messages to your clients relying upon the blunder, you can determine the blunder type after the aside from catchphrase. Have a go at running the program underneath.

attempt:

```
userInput1 = int(input("Please enter the number: ")) userInput2 = int(input("Please
enter another number: ")) answer =userInput1/userInput2
```

```
print ("The appropriate response is ", answer) myFile = open("missing.txt", 'r')
with the exception of ValueError:
```

```
print ("Error: You didn't enter a number") with the exception of
ZeroDivisionError: print ("Error: Cannot isolate by zero") aside from Exception as
e:
```

```
print ("Unknown mistake: ", e)
```

The rundown beneath demonstrates the different yields for various client inputs.
>>> signifies the client info and => indicates the yield.

>>> Please enter a number: m => Error: You didn't enter a number

Reason: User entered a string which can't be thrown into a whole number. This is
a ValueError. Henceforth, the statement in the aside from ValueError square is
shown.

>>> Please enter a number: 12

>>> Please enter another number: 0

=> Error: Cannot separate by zero

Reason: userInput2 = 0. Since we can't partition a number by zero, this is a
ZeroDivisionError. The statement in the aside from ZeroDivisionError square is
shown.

>>> Please enter a number: 12

>>> Please enter another number: 3

=> The appropriate response is 4.0

=> Unknown blunder: [Errno 2] No such record or index: 'missing.txt'

Reason: User enters worthy qualities and the line print ("The appropriate response
is ", answer) executes accurately. Nonetheless, the following line raises a mistake

as missing.txt isn't found. Since this isn't a ValueError or a ZeroDivisionError, the last aside from square is executed.

ValueError and ZeroDivisionError are two of the numerous pre-characterized blunder types in Python. ValueError is brought when a developed in activity or capacity gets a parameter that has the correct kind however a wrong worth. ZeroDivisionError is raised when the program attempts to isolate by zero. Other regular mistakes in Python incorporate

IOError

Raised when an I/O activity/operation, (for example, the inherent open() work) falls flat for an I/O-related explanation, e.g., "document not found".

ImportError:
Raised when an import statement neglects to discover the module definition
IndexError:

Raised when a grouping (for example string, list, tuple) file is out of range.

KeyError:
Raised when a lexicon key isn't found.

NameError:
Raised when a nearby or worldwide name isn't found.

TypeError:
Raised when an activity or capacity is applied to an object of unseemly kind.
For a total rundown of all the blunder types in Python, you can allude to https://docs.python.org/3/library/exceptions.html.

Python likewise accompanies pre-characterized mistake messages for every one of the various sorts of blunders. In the event that you need to show the message, you utilize the as watchword after the mistake type. For example, to show the default ValueError message, you compose:

with the exception of ValueError as e: print (e)
e is the variable name relegated to the mistake. You can give it some different names, however it is regular practice to utilize e. The last with the exception of statement in our program
but Exception as e:

print ("Unknown mistake: ", e) is a case of utilizing the pre-characterized mistake message. It fills in as a last endeavor to get any unexpected mistakes.

Chapter 7: Sets

A set type is **a group** of unique elements. Although a set itself is mutable, its elements must be immutable. Sets are used to carry out math operations involving sets such as intersection, union, or symmetric difference.

Creating a Set

You can create a set by enclosing all elements in curly braces {} or by using set(), one of Python's built-in functions. A set can hold items of different data types such as float, tuple, string, or integer. It cannot, however, hold a mutable element such as a dictionary, list, or set. Sets can hold any number of items. A comma is used to separate items from each other.

An example of s set of integers:

>>>my_set = {1, 4, 6, 8, 9, 10}

An example of a set of strings:

>>>my_set = {'a', 'e', 'i', 'o', 'u'}

An example of a set of mixed data types:
>>> my_set = {5.0, "Python", (5, 4, 2), 6}

An example of a set created from a list:

>>>set([5,4,3, 1])
{1, 3, 4, 5}
>>>

A set's elements cannot have a duplicate. When you create a set, Python evaluates if there are duplicates and drops the duplicate item.

Example #1:

>>> my_set = {'apple', 'peach', 'grape', 'apple', 'strawberry', 'grape'}
>>>my_set
{'peach', 'grape', 'apple', 'strawberry'}
>>>

68

Example #2:
```
>>>{1, 3, 5, 9, 1, 4, 3}
{1, 3, 4, 5, 9}
>>>
```

```
>>>set(['a', 'c', 'd', 'a', 'g', 'h', 'd'])
{'a', 'c', 'h', 'g', 'd'}
>>>
```

To create an empty set, you will have to use the set() function without an argument. You cannot use empty curly braces as this is the syntax for creating an empty dictionary.

```
>>> my_set = set()
>>>type(my_set)
<class 'set'>
>>>
```

Changing Elements on a Set

Sets are mutable so you can change their elements. Because sets are unordered, you cannot access or change an item or items through indexing or slicing like what you did earlier with strings and lists. You can, however, change the elements of a set with the methods **add()** or **update()**. The method add() appends a single element to a set while update() adds multiple elements. Strings, lists, tuples, or other sets can be used as argument when you use the update() method.

Example #1:

```
>>> my_set = {2, 4, 6, 8, 10}
>>> my_set.add(12)
>>> my_set
{2, 4, 6, 8, 10, 12}
>>>
```

Example #2:

```
>>> my_set = {2, 4, 6, 8, 10}
>>> my_set.update([14, 16, 18, 20])
>>> my_set
{2,4,6,8,10,12,14,16,18,20}
```

69

```
>>>
```

Example #3:

```
>>> my_set = {2, 4, 6, 8, 10}
>>> my_set.update('a', 'b')
>>> my_set
```

```
{2, 'a', 4, 6, 8, 10, 'b'}
>>>
```

Removing Set Elements

The **remove()** and **discard()** methods can be used to remove a specific item from a set. The only difference between the methods is their response to a non-existent argument. The use of the remove() method raises an error when the item given as argument does not exist. With discard(), the set simply remains unchanged.

Example #1:

```
>>> my_set = {'a', 'b', 'c', 'd', 'e', 'f', 'g'}
>>> my_set.discard('c')
>>> my_set
{'b', 'e', 'f', 'g', 'a', 'd'}
>>>
```

Example #2:
```
>>> my_set = {'a', 'b', 'c', 'd', 'e', 'f', 'g'}
>>> my_set.remove('f')
>>> my_set
{'e', 'd', 'b', 'c', 'a', 'g'}
>>>
```

Here is how Python responds when you use discard() with an item which is not foundon the set:

```
>>> my_set = {'a', 'b', 'c', 'd', 'e', 'f', 'g'}
>>> my_set.discard('x')
>>> my_set
```

{'g', 'd', 'e', 'c', 'a', 'f', 'b'}
>>>

The elements on the set were unchanged and no error was raised.

On the other hand, remove() will raise a Key Error if the item given as an argument is non-existent:

>>> my_set = {'a', 'b', 'c', 'd', 'e', 'f', 'g'}
>>> my_set.remove('x')
Traceback (most recent call last):
File "<pyshell#21>", line 1, in <module> my_set.remove('x')
KeyError: 'x'
>>>

The **pop()** method is likewise used to remove and return an item on a set. Since the **set is unordered**, you cannot possibly control which item will be popped. Selection is arbitrary.

>>> my_set = {'a', 'e', 'i', 'o', 'u'}
>>> my_set.pop()
'o'
>>> my_set
{'e', 'a', 'i', 'u'}
>>>

Now you can use the **clear()** method to remove all elements on a set.

>>> my_set = {'a', 'e', 'i', 'o', 'u'}
>>> my_set.clear()
>>> my_set set()
>>>

Set Operations

You can utilize sets to perform various set operations. To do this, you will use different Python operators or methods.

Set Union

A union of two sets refers to a set that contains all elements from the given sets. You can use the | **operator** or the **union()** method to perform the operation. The result is a combination of all elements which are returned in an **ascending order.**

Example with the | operator:

```
>>> x = {1,3,5,7,9,11,13}
>>> y = {2,4,6,8,10,12,14}
>>> x | y{1,2,3,4,5,6,7,8,9,10,11,12,13,14}
>>>
Example with the union() method:
>>> x = {1,3,5,7,9,11,13}
>>> y = {2,4,6,8,10,12,14}
>>> x.union(y)
{1,2,3,4,5,6,7,8,9,10,11,12,13,14}
>>>
```

Or

```
>>> x = {1,3,5,7,9,11,13}
>>> y = {2,4,6,8,10,12,14}
>>> y.union(X)
{1,2,3,4,5,6,7,8,9,10,11,12,13,14}
>>>
```

Set Intersection

The intersection of two different sets refers to the **set of common elements between them**. It is performed with either the **& operator** or the **intersection()** **method**. Both return a set with elements that are arranged in **ascending order**:
Example with the & operator:

```
>>> x = {1, 3, 5, 7, 2, 4, 6}
>>> y = {2, 4, 5, 7, 2, 0, 9}
>>> x & y
{2, 4, 5, 7}
>>>
```

Example with the intersection() method:

```
>>> x = {1, 3, 5, 7, 2, 4, 6}
>>> y = {2, 4, 5, 7, 2, 0, 9}
>>> x.intersection(y)
{2, 4, 5, 7}
>>> y.intersection(x)
{2, 4, 5, 7}
>>>
```

Set Difference

Set difference refers to a set of elements that are found in one set but not in the other set. For instance, the difference of X and Y (X – Y) is a set of elements that can be found in X but not in Y. Conversely, the difference of Y and X (Y – X) is a set of elements that are found in Y but not in X. The set difference operation is performed with either the – **operator** or the **difference() method**.

Examples with the - operator:

```
>>> x = {1, 2, 3, 5, 7, 9}
>>> y = {2, 8, 9, 5, 2, 1}
>>> x - y
{3, 7}
>>> y - x
{8}
>>>
```

Examples with the difference() method:

```
>>> x = {1, 2, 3, 5, 7, 9}
>>> y = {2, 8, 9, 5, 2, 1}
>>> x.difference(y)
{3, 7}
>>> y.difference(x)
{8}
>>>
```

Set Symmetric Difference

The symmetric difference between two sets refers to the set of elements that are not common in both sets. It is performed with either the ^ **operator** or the **symmetric_difference() method**.
Example with the ^ operator:
```
>>> a = {1, 3, 5, 4, 6, 8}
>>> b = {5, 2, 6, 1, 8, 10}
>>> a ^ b
{2, 3, 4, 10}
>>>
```

Examples with the symmetric_difference() method:

```
>>> a = {1, 3, 5, 4, 6, 8}
>>> b = {5, 2, 6, 1, 8, 10}
>>> a.symmetric_difference(b)
{2, 3, 4, 10}
>>> b.symmetric_difference(a)
{2, 3, 4, 10}
>>>
```

Set Membership Test

The **membership test operators**(the "in" and "not in" operators) can be used to test the existence or non-existence of an item on a set.

For example:

```
>>> my_set = {'land', 'sea', 'air', 'ocean', 'river'}
>>>'sea'in my_set True
>>>'river'not in my_set False
>>>
```

Using Built-in Functions with Set
There are several Python functions that are often used with set to carry out various tasks.

Len()
Returns the number of elements on a set.

```
>>>my_set = {1, 'a', 2, 'b', 3, 'c'}
>>>len(my_set) 6
>>>
```

Max()
Returns the largest element on a set.

```
>>>my_set = {1,2,3,4,5}
>>>max(my_set) 5
>>>
```

On a set of strings, max() returns the last item alphabetical-wise.

```
>>> b = {'a', 'b', 'c', 'd', 'e'}
>>>max(b) 'e'
>>>
```

Min()
Returns the smallest element on a set.
```
>>> a = {2, 1, 5, 8, 9, 20}
>>>min(a) 1
>>>
>>> b = {'a', 'b', 'c', 'd', 'e'}
>>>min(b) 'a'
>>>
```

Sorted()
Returns a sorted list of set elements but does not actually sort the set.

Chapter 8: Functions and Modules

Earlier in this book, we've briefly mentioned functions and modules. In this chapter, we will look at them in detail. Once again, all programming languages come with built-in codes that we can utilize to make our lives easier as programmers. These codes usually are made up of pre-written classes, variables and functions for performing certain common tasks and are saved in files known as modules. Let's first look at functions.

What are Functions?

Functions can be simply defined pre-written codes that perform a certain task. For an analogy, think of the mathematical functions available in MS Excel. To add numbers, we can use the sum() function and type sum(A1:A5) instead of typing A1+A2+A3+A4+A5.

Depending on the way function is written, whether it is part of a class (a class is a concept in object-oriented programming which we be discussed in advanced book) and how do you import it, we can call a function by simply typing the name of the function or by using the dot notation. Some functions require us to transfer data in for them to perform their tasks. These data are known as parameters and we pass them to the function by enclosing their values in parenthesis ( ) separated by commas.

For example, to utilize the print() function for displaying text on the screen, we will call it by typing print("Hello World") where print is the name of the function and "Hello World" is the parameter.

On the opposite hand, to use the change() function for manipulating text strings, we've get to type 'Hello World'.replace("World", "Universe") , here change is the name of the function and "World" and "Universe" are the parameters. The string before the dot (i.e. 'Hello World') is will be changed as a string. Hence, 'Hello World' will be turned to 'Hello Universe'.

Defining Your Own Functions

We can define our personal functions in Python to reuse them throughout the program. The step for defining a function is as below:

deffunctionName(parameters): code detailing what the function should do return [expression]

There are two keywords here, def and return.

deftells the program that the indented code from the next line onwards is part of the function. return is that keyword that we tend to return an answer from the function. There is possibility of more than one return statements in a function. However, once the function carries out a return statement, the function will exit. If your function does not require to return any value, you can leave out the return statement. Instead, you can just write return or return None.

Let us now define our first function. Suppose we want to determine if a given number is a prime number. Here's how we can define the function using the modulus (%) operator.

def checkIfPrime (numberToCheck): for x in range(2, numberToCheck): if (numberToCheck%x ==0):
return False return True

In the above function, lines 2 and 3 uses a forloop to divide the given parameter numberToCheckby all numbers from 2to numberToCheck
- 1 to determine if the remainder is zero. If the remainder is zero, numberToCheck is not a prime number. Line 4 will give back False and the function will exit.

If through last iteration of the forloop, none of the division has a remainder of zero, the function will reach Line 5, and return True. Then, the function will then exit.

To use this function, we type checkIfPrime(13)and assign it to a variable like this
answer = checkIfPrime(13)

In this condition we are passing in 13 as the parameter. We can go ahead to print the answer by typing print(answer). We'll get the output: True.

Variable Scope

A very important concept to understand when defining a function is the concept of variable scope. Variables that defined inside of a function are treated differently from variables defined outside of it. There are two main differences.

Firstly, any variable declared <u>inside</u> a function is only accessible within the function. These are known as local variables. Any variable that is declared outside a function is known as a global variable and is accessible anywhere in the program.

To understand this, try the code below:
```
message1 = "Global Variable"

def myFunction():
        print("\nINSIDE THE FUNCTION") #Global variables are accessible
inside a function print (message1)
        #Declaring a local variable message2 = "Local Variable"
print (message2)


#Calling the function myFunction() print("\nOUTSIDE THEFUNCTION")
#Global variables are accessible outside function print (message1)

#Local variables are NOT accessible outside function. print (message2)
```

If you run the program, you will get the output below.

INSIDE THE FUNCTION
Global
Variable
Local
Variable

OUTSIDE THE FUNCTION
Global Variable
NameError: name 'message2' is notdefined

78

Within the function, both the local and global variables are accessible. Outside the function, the local variable message2 is no longer accessible. We get a NameErrorwhen we try to get access to it outside the function.

The second concept to understand about variable scope is that if a local variable shares the same name as a global variable, any code <u>inside</u> the function is accessing the <u>local</u> variable. Any code <u>outside</u> is accessing the <u>global</u> variable. Try to run the code below
message1 = 'Global Variable (shares the same name as a local variable)'

```
defmyFunction():
        message1 = 'Local Variable (shares same name as a global variable)'
        print("\nINSIDETHEFUNCTION") print (message1)
```

Calling the function myFunction()

Printing message1 OUTSIDE the function print ("\nOUTSIDE THE FUNCTION") print(message1)

You'll get the output as follows:
INSIDE THE FUNCTION
Local Variable (shares same name as a global variable) OUTSIDE THE FUNCTION
Global Variable (shares same name as a local variable)
When message is printed the function, it prints "Local

Variable (shares same name as a global variable)" as it is printing the local variable. When we print it outside, it is accessing the global variable and hence prints "Global Variable (shares same name as a local variable)".

Importing Modules

Python basically comes with quite a large number of built-in functions. These built-in functions are saved in files known as modules. To utilize the built-in codes in Python modules, we have to import them into our programs first. We do that by using the importkeyword. There are three ways to do it.
The first way is to import the entire module by writing import moduleName.

For example, to import the randommodule, we write importrandom. Touse the randrange() function in the random module, we write random.randrange(1, 10).

If you find it too tedious or stressful to write random each time you use the function, you can import the module by writing import random as r (where r is any name of your choice). Now to use the randrange() function, you simply write r.randrange(1, 10).

The third way to import modules is to import specific functions from the module by writing from moduleName import name1[, name2[, ... nameN]].

For instance, to import the randrange() function from the random module, we write from random import randrange. If we want to import and use more than 1 functions, we separate them with a comma. To import the randrange() and randint() functions, we write from random import randrange, randint. To utilize the function now, we do not have to use the dot notation any longer. Just write randrange(1, 10).

Creating our Own Module

Apart from importing built-in modules, we can also create our personal modules. This is terribly helpful if you have got some functions that you simply need to apply in alternative programming comes in future.

Creating a module is simple. Just save the file with a .py extension and place it in the same folder as the Python file that you are going to import it from.

Suppose you want to use the checkIfPrime() function defined earlier in another Python script. Here's how you do it. To begin with, save the code above as prime.py on your desktop. prime.py should contain the following code.

```
def checkIfPrime (numberToCheck): for x in range(2, numberToCheck):
if (numberToCheck%x ==0): return False
return True
```

Next, you should prepare another Python file and name it useCheckIfPrime.py.

Save it on your desktop as well. useCheckIfPrime.py should have the following code.

```
import prime
answer  =  prime.checkIfPrime(13)
print (answer)
```

Now run useCheckIfPrime.py. You should get the output True. Simple as that.

However, assuming you want to store prime.py and use CheckIfPrime.py in a number different folders. You are going to have to add some codes to use CheckIfPrime.py to tell the Python interpreter where to find the module.

Say you created a folder named 'MyPythonModules' in your C drive to store prime.py. You need to add the following code to the top of your useCheckIfPrime.py file (before the line import prime).

```
import sys
```

```
if          'C:\\MyPythonModules'          not          in          sys.path:
sys.path.append('C:\\MyPythonModules')
```

sys.path refers to your Python's system path. That is the list of directories that Python scans through to search for modules and files. The above code also appends the folder 'C:\MyPythonModules' to your system path.

Now, you can place prime.py in C:\MyPythonModules and checkIfPrime.py in any other folder of your choice.

Chapter 9: Using Files

Very good! Now we reached the last chapter, before the project. We'll now look at how we can work with external files.

We've seen how to we can get input from the user using input(). But, sometimes, if we need to work with a lot of data, it's more common to use files instead of manual inputs.
This chapter will teach you how!

Reading Files

In this first example, we are going to read from a plain text file. Let's start: create a file with the following text.

Learn Python and Learn It Well

Save this file as myfile.txt in your desktop. Then,open IDLE and write the code below. Save this file as fileOperation.py, again on your desktop.

```
f = open ('myfile.txt', 'r')
firstline = f.readline()
secondline = f.readline()
print (firstline)
print (secondline) f.close()
```

The first line has a specific function: open the file.
Before reading from any file, we must open it. The open() function does exactly that.

The 1st parameter is simply the file path.
In case you didn't keep fileOperation.py and myfile.txt in the same directory, you'll need to add, before 'myfile.txt', the full path where you stored the text file. For example, if you saved it in a folder named 'PythonFiles' in your C drive, you need to code 'C:\\PythonFiles\\myfile.txt'.

The other parameter is the file open mode. Commonly used modes are

'r' mode:

For reading only.

'w' mode:
For writing only.

If the desired file doesn't exist, it'll be now created.
If the specified file already exists, existing data on the file will be erased and you'll start with a plain one.

'a' mode:
To append.

If the desired file doesn't exist, it'll be now created.
If the specified file already exists, existing data on the file will be kept and you'll start writing at the bottom of the file.

'r+' mode:
For reading and writing.

After you open the file, the following code

firstline = f.readline()
Is useful to read the first line in the file and assign it to the variable.

Everytime time the readline() function is called, it reads a new line from the file.
In our program, readline() was called two times. So the first two lines will be read.

You'll find that a line break is inserted after every line you write in the file.
This is caused by the readline() function: it automatically adds the '\n' characters to the end of each line. In case you don't want that double line between each line of text, you can execute
print (firstline, end = '').

This will remove the new line characters for the following output.
After reading and printing the two lines, the last line, f.close(), simply closes the file.
You should always close the file once you're done accessing it, so the system can free up some system resources.

Read files with a loop

The readline() function we described above to read a text file, is not enough to read a file with a undefinied row number.
The solution is a loop: here's how you can do that.

```
f = open ("myfile.txt",'r')
for line in f:
 print (line, end = '')
f.close()
```

As you can guess, the loop cycles through the text file, line by line.

Writing to a File

Now that we've discovered how to open and read a file, let's move on and start writing into it.

To do so, we'll use the append mode, identified with 'a'.
It's also possible to use the 'w' mode, that will erase and replace all the content of the file.

```
f = open ('myfile.txt', 'a')
f.write('\nAny new row will be appended.')
f.write('\nHere is it!')
f.close()
```

Now we use the write() function to append the two sentences to the file, each starting on a new line entirely because we used the escape characters '\n'.

Challenge Yourself

We've come to the end of this chapter and hopefully you have successfully coded your first program. If you have problems solving any exercise, you can study the answers in Appendix E. You'll learn a lot by taking your time to study other people's codes.

In this section, I have three additional exercises for you to challenge yourself.

Challenge Exercise 1
In the program that we've coded so far, I've avoided using the division operator. Can you modify the program so that it will create questions with the division sign too? How would you check the user's answer against the correct answer?

Hint: Check out the round() function.

Challenge Exercise 2
Sometimes, the question generated may result in an answer that is very large or very small. For example, the question 6*[8^9/1]^3 will give the answer 1450710985375550096474112.
It is very uncomfortable for users to calculate and put in such a large number. Hence, we want to avoid answers that are too big or small. Can you edit the program to prevent questions that brings out answers greater than 50 000 or smaller than -50000?

Challenge Exercise 3

The last challenge exercise is the most difficult.

So far, brackets are missing in the questions generated. Can you modify the program so that the questions use brackets too? An example of a question will be 2 + (3*7 -1) + 5.

Have fun with these exercises. The suggested solution is provided in Appendix E.

Appendix A: Working With Strings

Note: The notation (start,(end))means start and end are choosen parameters. If only one number is provided as the parameter, it is taken to be start.

marks the start of a comment
''' signifies the start and end of a multiline comment. The actual code is in monotype font.

=> marks the start of the output
count (sub, [start, [end]])
Return the number of times the substring sub appears in the string. This function is case-sensitive.

[Example]
In the examples below. 's' occurs at index 3 ,6 and10 # count the entire string
'This is a string'.count('s')
=> 3
count from index 4 to end of string 'This is a string'.count('s', 4) => 2 # count from index 4 to 10-1
'This is a string'. count('s', 4, 10) => 1

count 'T'. There's only one 'T' as the function is case sensitive.
'This is a string'. count('T')
=> 1

endswith (suffix, [start, [end]])
Return the True if the string comes to an end with the specified suffix, otherwise return False.
suffix can also be a tuple of suffixes to search for. This function is case-sensitive.

[Example]
"man"occurs at index 4 to 6# check the entire string
'Postman'.ends with('man')
=> True

check From the index 3 to end of string 'Postman'.ends with('man', 3)
=> True

check from index 2 to 6-1
'Postman'.endswith('man', 2, 6) => False

check from index 2 to 7-1
'Postman'.endswith('man', 2, 7) => True

Using a tuple of suffixes 'Postman'. ends with (('man', 'ma'), 2, 6) => True

find/index (sub, [start, [end]])
Return the index in the string where the first occurrence of the substring
sub is found.
find() returns -1 if sub is not found.
index() returns ValueError is sub is not found. This function is case-sensitive.

[Example]
check the entire string
'This is a string'.find('s')
=> 3
check from index 4 to end of string 'This is a string'.find('s', 4) => 6 # check
from index 7 to 11-1
'This is a string'.find('s', 7,11) => 10

Sub is not found
'This is a string'.find('p')
=> -1

'This is a string'.index('p')
=> ValueError

isalnum()

Return the true if all characters in the string are alphanumerics and there is at least
one character, false the otherwise.
Alphanumeric does not include whitespaces.
[Example]
'abcd1234'.isalnum()
=> True

'a b c d 1 2 3 4'.isalnum()
=> False

'abcd'.isalnum()
=> True

'1234'.isalnum()
=> True

isalpha()
Return the true if all the characters in the string are in alphabet format and there is at least one character, false the otherwise.

[Example]

'abcd'.isalpha()
=> True

'abcd1234'.isalpha()
=> False

'1234'.isalpha()
=> False

'a b c'.isalpha()
=> False

isdigit()

Return the true if all the characters in the string are all digits and there is at least one character, false the otherwise.

[Example]

'1234'.isdigit()
=> True
'abcd1234'.isdigit()
=> False

'abcd'.isdigit()
=> False

'1 2 3 4'.isdigit()
=> False

islower()

Return the true if all cased characters in the string are lowercase and there is at least one cased character, false otherwise.

[Example]

'abcd'.islower()
=> True

'Abcd'.islower()
=> False

'ABCD'.islower()
=> False

isspace()
Return the true if all are only whitespace characters in the string and there is at least one character, false otherwise.

[Example]

' '.isspace()
=> True

'a b'.isspace()
=> False

istitle()
Return the true if the string is a titlecased string and there is at least one character
[Example]

'This Is A String'.istitle()
=> True

'This is a string'.istitle()
=> False
isupper()
Return true if all cased characters in the string are all uppercase and there is at least one cased character, false otherwise.

[Example]

'ABCD'.isupper()
=> True

'Abcd'.isupper()
=> False

'abcd'.isupper()

=> False
join()

Return a single string in which the parameter given is joined by a separator.
[Example]
sep = '-'
myTuple = ('a', 'b', 'c')
myList = ['d', 'e', 'f'] myString = "Hello World"

sep.join(myTuple)
=> 'a-b-c'

sep.join(myTuple)
=> 'd-e-f'

sep.join(myString)
=> 'H-e-l-l-o- -W-o-r-l-d''

lower()

Return a single copy of the string converted to the lowercase. [Example]
'Hello Python'.lower()
=> 'hello python'

replace(old, new[, count])

Return a single copy of the string with all occurrences of substring old replaced by new.
count is optional. If given, only the first count occurrences are replaced. This function is case-sensitive.

[Example]

Replace all occurences
'This is a string'.replace('s', 'p') => 'Thip ip a ptring'

Replace first 2 occurences
'This is a string'.replace('s', 'p', 2) => 'Thip ip a string'

split([sep [,maxsplit]])

Return a single list of the words in the string, using the sep as the delimiter string. sep and maxsplit are optional.
If sep is not given, whitespace is used as the delimiter. if maxsplit is provided, at most maxsplit are done.
This function is case-sensitive. [Example]
'''
Split using comma (,) as the delimiter signal that there's a space provided before the words 'is', 'a' and 'string' in the outcome.
'''
"This, is, a, string". split(',') => ['This', ' is', ' a', ' string']

Split using whitespace as delimiter 'This is a string'.split()

=> ['This', 'is', 'a', 'string']

Only do 2 splits
'This, is, a,. "string". split(',' 2) => ['This', ' is', ' a, string']

splitlines ([keepends])

Return a single list of the lines in the string, breaking at the line boundaries.
Linebreaks are not mentioned in the resulting list unless keep ends is provided and true.

[Example]

Split lines separated by \n
'This is the first line.\nThis is the second line'.splitlines() => ['This is the first line.', 'This is the second line.']

Split multi line string (e.g. string that uses the "mark)" 'This is the first line.

This is the second line.'''.splitlines() => ['This is the first line.', 'This is the second line.']

Split and keep line breaks
'This is the first line.\nThis is the second line.'.splitlines(True) => ['This is the first line.\n', 'This is the second line.']

'''This is the first line.
This is the second line.'''.splitlines(True) => ['This is the first line.\n', 'This is the second line.']
startswith (prefix[, start[, end]])

Return the True if string starts with the prefix, or otherwise return False.
prefix could also be a tuple of prefixes to look for. This function is case-sensitive.

[Example]
'Post' occurs at index 0 to 3 # check the entire string
'Postman'.startswith('Post')
=> True

check from index 3 to end of string 'Postman'.startswith('Post', 3) =>
False

check from index 2 to 6-1
'Postman'.startswith('Post', 2, 6) => False

check from index 2 to 6-1
'Postman'.startswith('stm', 2, 6) => True

Using a tuple of prefixes (check from index 3 to end of string)
'Postman'.startswith(('Post', 'tma'), 3) => True

strip ([chars])
Return a single copy of the string with the leading and trailing characters char removed.
If char is not provided, whitespaces will be removed. This function is case-sensitive.

[Example]

Strip whitespaces

92

' This, is, a, string '.strip() => 'This is a string'

Strip 's'. Nothing is removed since 's' is not at the start or end of the string 'This is a string'.strip('s')
=> 'This is a string'

Strip 'g'.
'This is a string'.strip('g')
=> 'This is a strin'

upper()
Return a single copy of the string converted to uppercase. [Example]
'Hello Python'.upper()
=> 'HELLO PYTHON'

Appendix B: Working With Lists

=> marks the start of the output
append( )
Add item to the end of a list
[Example]

myList = ['a', 'b', 'c', 'd'] myList.append('e') print (myList)
=> ['a', 'b', 'c', 'd', 'e']

del
Remove items from a list
[Example]

myList = ['a', 'b', 'c', 'd', 'e', 'f', 'g', 'h', 'i', 'j', 'k', 'l']

#delete the third item (index = 2) del myList[2]
print (myList)
=> ['a','b','d','e','f','g','h','i','j','k','l']

#delete items from index 1 to 5-1
del myList[1:5] print (myList)
=> ['a', 'g', 'h', 'i', 'j', 'k', 'l']

#delete items from index 0 to 3-1
del myList [:3] print (myList)
=> ['i', 'j', 'k', 'l']

#delete items from index 2 to end del myList [2:]
print (myList)
=> ['i', 'j']

extend( )
Combine two lists
[Example]
myList = ['a', 'b', 'c', 'd', 'e'] myList2 = [1, 2, 3, 4]
myList.extend(myList2) print (myList)
=> ['a', 'b', 'c', 'd', 'e', 1, 2, 3, 4]

In
Check if an item is in a list
[Example]

myList = ['a', 'b', 'c', 'd'] 'c' in myList
=> True

'e' in myList
=> False

insert( )
Add item to a list at a particular position
 [Example]
myList = ['a', 'b', 'c', 'd', 'e'] myList.insert(1, 'Hi') print (myList)
=> ['a', 'Hi', 'b', 'c', 'd', 'e']

len( )
Find the number of items in a list [Example]

myList = ['a', 'b', 'c', 'd'] print (len(myList)) => 4
pop( )
Get the value of an item and remove it from the list Requires index of item as the
parameter

[Example]

myList = ['a', 'b', 'c', 'd', 'e']

#remove the third item member = myList.pop(2) print (member)
=> c

print (myList)
=> ['a', 'b', 'd', 'e']

#remove the last item member = myList.pop( ) print (member)
=> e

print (myList)
=> ['a', 'b', 'd']

remove( )
Remove an item from a list. Requires the value of the item as the parameter.

[Example]

myList = ['a', 'b', 'c', 'd', 'e']

#remove the item 'c'
myList.remove('c') print (myList)
=> ['a', 'b', 'd', 'e']

reverse()
Reverse the items in a list
[Example]

myList = [1, 2, 3, 4] myList.reverse() print (myList)
=> [4, 3, 2, 1]

sort()
Sort a list alphabetically or numerically
[Example]

myList = [3, 0, -1, 4, 6]
myList.sort() print(myList)
=> [-1, 0, 3, 4, 6]

sorted()
Return a new sorted list without sorting the original list.
Requires a list as the parameter [Example]

myList = [3, 0, -1, 4, 6]
myList2 = sorted(myList)
#Original list is not sorted print (myList)
=> [3, 0, -1, 4, 6]

#New list is sorted print (myList2)
=> [-1, 0, 3, 4, 6]

Addition Operator: +
Concatenate List [Example]
myList = ['a', 'b', 'c', 'd']
print (myList + ['e', 'f']) => ['a', 'b', 'c', 'd', 'e', 'f']

print (myList)
=> ['a', 'b', 'c', 'd']

Multiplication Operator: *
Duplicate a list and concatenate it to the end of the list [Example]

myList = ['a', 'b', 'c', 'd'] print (myList*3)

=> ['a', 'b', 'c', 'd', 'a', 'b', 'c', 'd', 'a', 'b', 'c', 'd']

print (myList)
=> ['a', 'b', 'c', 'd']

Note:
**The + and * symbols do not modify the list. The list stays as ['a', 'b', 'c','d']
in both cases.**

Appendix C: Working With Tuples

=> marks the start of the output
del
Delete the entire tuple
[Example]

myTuple = ('a', 'b', 'c', 'd') del myTuple
print (myTuple) => NameError: name 'myTuple' is not defined

in
Check if an item is in a tuple [Example]

myTuple = ('a', 'b', 'c', 'd') 'c' in myTuple => True 'e' in myTuple => False
len( )
Find the number of items in a tuple [Example]

myTuple = ('a', 'b', 'c', 'd') print (len(myTuple)) => 4

Addition Operator: +
Concatenate Tuples
[Example]

myTuple = ('a', 'b', 'c', 'd') print (myTuple + ('e',
'f')) => ('a', 'b', 'c', 'd', 'e', 'f')
print (myTuple) => ('a', 'b', 'c', 'd')

Multiplication Operator: *
Duplicate a tuple and concatenate it to the end of the tuple [Example]

myTuple = ('a', 'b', 'c', 'd') print(myTuple*3) => ('a', 'b', 'c', 'd', 'a', 'b', 'c', 'd', 'a',
'b', 'c', 'd')
print (myTuple) => ('a', 'b', 'c', 'd')

Note: The + and * symbols do not modify the tuple. The tuple stays as ['a', 'b',
'c', 'd'] in both cases.

Appendix D: Working With Dictionaries

=> marks the start of the output

clear( )
Removes all elements of the dictionary, returning an empty dictionary [Example]

dic1 = {1: 'one', 2: 'two'} print (dic1)

=> {1: 'one', 2: 'two'}

dic1.clear() print (dic1)
=> { }

del
Delete the entire dictionary [Example]

dic1 = {1: 'one', 2: 'two'} del dic1
print (dic1)
=> NameError: name 'dic1' is not defined

get( )
Returns a value for the given key.
If the key is not found, it'll return the keyword None.
Alternatively, you can state the value to return if the key is not found.
[Example]
dic1 = {1: 'one', 2: 'two'} dic1.get(1)
=> 'one'

dic1.get(5)
=> None

dic1.get(5, "Not Found") => 'Not Found'

In
Check if an item is in a dictionary [Example]

dic1 = {1: 'one', 2: 'two'}

based on the key 1 in dic1
=> True

3 in dic1
=> False

based on the value 'one' in dic1.values() => True 'three' in dic1.values() =>
False **items( )**
Returns a list of dictionary's pairs as tuples

[Example]
dic1 = {1: 'one', 2: 'two'} dic1.items()
=> dict_items([(1, 'one'), (2, 'two')])

keys( )

Returns list of the dictionary's keys [Example]

dic1 = {1: 'one', 2: 'two'} dic1.keys()
=> dict_keys([1, 2])

len( )
Find the number of items in a dictionary [Example]

dic1 = {1: 'one', 2: 'two'} print (len(dic1)) => 2

update( )

Adds one dictionary's key-values pairs to another. Duplicates are removed.

[Example]

dic1 = {1: 'one', 2: 'two'}
dic2 = {1: 'one', 3: 'three'}

dic1.update(dic2) print (dic1)
=> {1: 'one', 2: 'two', 3: 'three'}

print (dic2) #no change => {1: 'one', 3: 'three'}

values( )
Returns list of the dictionary's values [Example]

dic1 = {1: 'one', 2: 'two'} dic1.values()
=> dict_values(['one', 'two'])

Appendix E: Project Answers

Exercise 1

```
from random import randint from os import remove, rename
```

Exercise 2

```
def getUserScore(userName):

try:
input = open('userScores.txt', 'r') for line in input:
content = line.split(',') if content[0] == userName:
input.close() return content[1]
input.close() return "-1"
except IOError:
print ("\nFile userScores.txt not found. a new file will be made.'). input =
 open('userScores.txt', 'w')
input.close() return "-1"
```

Exercise 3

```
def updateUserPoints(newUser, userName, score): if newUser:
input = open('userScores.txt', 'a') input.write('\n' + userName + ', ' + score)
input.close()
else:
input = open('userScores.txt', 'r') output = open('userScores.tmp', 'w')
for line in input:
content = line.split(',') if content[0] == userName:
content[1] = score
line = content[0] +','+content[1] + '\n'

output.write(line) input.close() output.close()


remove('userScores.txt') rename('userScores.tmp', 'userScores.txt')
```

Exercise 4

```
def generateQuestion():
operandList = [0, 0, 0, 0, 0] operatorList = ['', '', '', '']
operatorDict = {1:'+',2:' -', 3:'',4:'*'}
```

```
for index in range(0, 5): operandList[index] = randint(1, 9)

for index in range(0, 4):
if index > 0 and operatorList[index-1] != '**': operator = operatorDict[randint(1,
4)]
else: operator = operatorDict[randint(1, 3)]
operatorList[index] = operator questionString = str(operandList[0])

for index in range(1, 5): questionString = questionString +
operatorList[index-1] + str(operandList[index]) result = eval(questionString)

questionString = questionString.replace("**", "^") print ('\n' + questionString)

userResult = input('Answer: ')
while True:
try:
if int(userResult) == result:
print . ('So Smart') return 1 else: print ("Sorry, wrong
answer. The correct answer is", result)
return 0
Remove Exception as e: print ("You did not enter a number. Please try again.")
userResult = input('Answer: ')
```

[Explanation for Exercise 9.2]

Starting from the second item (i.e. index = 1) in operatorList, the line if index > 0 and operatorList[index-1] != '**': checks if the previous item in operatorList is the '**' symbol..

If not, the statement operator = operator Dict[randint (1, 4)] will execute. Since the range given to the randint function is 1 to 4, the numbers 1, 2, 3 or 4 will be generated. Hence, the symbols '+', '-', '' or '*' will be assigned to the variable operator.

However, if the previous symbol is '**', the else statement (operator = operatorDict[randint(1, 3)]) will execute. In this case, the range given to the randint function is from 1 to 3. Hence, the '**' symbol, which has a key of 4 in operatorDict will NOT be assigned to the operator variable.

Exercise 5

```
try:

    import myPythonFunctions as m

    userName = input("'Please enter your user name or create a new one if this is the
first time you are running the program: '")

    userScore = int(m.getUserScore(userName)) if userScore == -1:
    newUser = True userScore = 0
    else:
    newUser = False
    userChoice = 0

    while userChoice != '-1':

        userScore += m.generateQuestion() print ("Current Score = ", userScore)
        userChoice = input("Press Enter To Continue or -1 to Exit: ")
        m.updateUserPoints(newUser, userName, str(userScore))
except Exception as e:
    print ("An unexpected error occurred. Program will be exited.")
```

Conclusion

Python is a powerful programming language and gives a simple use of the code lines, maintenance can be dealt with in an extraordinary manner, and debugging or investigation of code should be possible effectively as well. It has picked up significance over the globe as PC mammoth Google has made it one of its official programming languages.

So, we've come to the end of the book and I am sure this book will give you all that are required to jump on the python programming language and explore further.

Thank you for reading this book and I hope you have enjoyed the book. More importantly, I sincerely hope the book has helped you master the fundamentals of Python programming.

Python Advanced Programming - Chapter 1: Advanced Programming Techniques

In this Chapter we will investigate a wide scope of programming methodologies and present various extra, consistently further created, Python etymological structure. Bits of the material in this segment is very trying, yet recall that the most dynamic techniques are now and again required and you can commonly skim the primary go through to get an idea of what should be conceivable and scrutinized even more circumspectly when the need rises.

The part's first area delves all the more profoundly into Python's procedural highlights. It begins by telling the best way to utilize what we previously canvassed in a novel manner, and after that profits to the topic of generators. The segment at that point presents dynamic programming—stacking modules by name at runtime and executing self-assertive code at runtime. The area comes back to the subject of nearby (settled) capacities, however what's more covers the utilization of the nonlocal watchword and recursive capacities. Prior we perceived how to utilize Python's predefined decorators—in this segment we figure out how to make our own decorators. The area finishes up with inclusion of annotations.

The second part covers all new material relating to object-oriented program-ming. It starts by the introduction of __slots__, a mechanism to minimize the memory used by any object. Then, it shows how to access object attributes without using its properties.
The section also describes functors, and context managers—these are used in conjunction with the with keyword, and in many cases (e.g., file handling) they can be used to replace try ... except ... finally constructs with simpler try ... except constructs. Thesection also shows how to create custom context managers, and introduces additional advanced features, including class decorators, abstract base classes, multiple inheritance, and metaclasses.

The third area intoduces some basic concepts of functional programming, and presents some valuable functions from the functools, itertools,and administrator modules. This segment additionally tells the best way to utilize halfway capacity application to simplify code, and how to make and utilize co-routines.

This chapter takes everything that we have just covered and transforms it into the "deluxe Python toolbox", with all the first instruments (tech-niques and punctuations), in addition to numerous new ones that can make our programming simpler, shorter, and increasingly viable. A portion of the devices can have tradable uses, for instance, a few occupations should be possible utilizing either a class decorator or a metaclass, while others, for example, descriptors, can be utilized in various approaches to accomplish various impacts. A portion of the apparatuses secured here, for instance, setting supervisors, we will utilize constantly, and others will stay prepared close by for those specific circumstances for which they are the ideal arrangement.

Further Procedural Programming

The majority of this area manages additional facilities relating with procedural programming and functions, yet the absolute first subsection is diverse in that it shows a helpful programming system dependent on what we previously covered without presenting any new syntax.
Branching Using Dictionaries

As we noted before, functions are items like everything else in Python, and a function's name is an object reference that alludes to the functions. On the off chance that we compose a function's name without brackets, Python realizes we mean the reference, and we can transfer such references around simply like any others. We can utilize this reality to supplant if proclamations that have loads of elif provisions with a single function call.

We will obseve an intelligent console called dvds-dbm.py, featuring the following menu:

(A)dd (E)dit (L)ist (R)emove (I)mport e(X)port (Q)uit

The software has a function that gets the user's decision and which will return just a legitimate decision, for this situation one of "an", "e", "l", "r", "I", "x", and "q". Here are two proportional code pieces for calling the important functions dependent on the user's decision:

```
if action == "a":

    add_dvd(db)

elif action == "e":
```

```python
        edit_dvd(db)


    elif action == "l":

        list_dvds(db)

            elif action == "r":

            remove_dvd(db)

            elif action == "i":
                                    functions = dict(a=add_dvd, e=edit_dvd, l=list_dvds,
                                                     r=remove_dvd, i=import_,
            import_(db)                              x=export, q=quit)

    elif action == "x":                 functions[action](db)

        export(db)

    elif action == "q":

        quit(db)
```

The decision is held as a one-character string in the activity variable, and the database to be utilized is held in the db variable. The import_() function has a trailing underscore to keep it distinct from the built-in import proclamation.

In the correct hand code piece we make a lexicon whose keys are the legitimate menu decisions, and whose qualities are function references. In the second proclamation we recover the function reference comparing to the given activity and call the function alluded to utilizing the call administrator, (), and in this model, passing the db contention. Not exclusively is the code on the right-hand side a lot shorter than the code on the left, yet in addition it can scale (have unmistakably more word reference things) without influencing its performance, dissimilar to one side hand code whose speed relies upon what number of elifs must be tried to locate the suitable function to call.

The convert-incidents.py program uses this technique in its import_() method, as this extract from the method shows:

```
call = {(".aix", "dom"): self.import_xml_dom,

       (".aix", "etree"): self.import_xml_etree,

       (".aix", "sax"): self.import_xml_sax,

       (".ait", "manual"): self.import_text_manual,

       (".ait", "regex"): self.import_text_regex,

       (".aib", None): self.import_binary,

       (".aip", None): self.import_pickle}

result = call[extension, reader](filename)
```

The total method is 13 lines in length; the expansion parameter is processed in the method, and the reader is passed in. The word reference keys are 2-tuples, and the qualities are methods. On the off chance that we had utilized if statements, the code would be 22 lines in length, and would not scale also.

Generator Expressions and Functions

It is additionally conceivable to make generator expressions. These are syntactically nearly identical to list comprehensions, the distinction being that they are encased in paantheses instead of backets. Here are their syntaxes:

(*expression* for *item* in *iterable*)

(*expression* for *item* in *iterable* if *condition*)

Here are two equal code bits that show how a simple for ... in loop containing a yield articulation can be coded as a generator:

```
def items_in_key_order(d):            def items_in_key_order(d):

    for key in sorted(d):                 return ((key, d[key])

        yield key, d[key]                     for key in sorted(d))
```

Both functions return a generator that produces a list of key–value items for the given dictionary. If we need all the items in one go we can pass the generator returned by the

functions to list() or tuple(); otherwise, we can iterate over the generator to retrieve items as we need them.

Generators give a method for performing languid evaluation, which implies that they figure just the values that are really required. This can be more productive than, say, processing an extremely enormous rundown in one go. A few generators produce the same number of values as we request—with no upper limit. For instance:

```
def quarters(next_quarter=0.0):
```

```
while True:

    yield next_quarter

    next_quarter += 0.25
```

This function will return 0.0, 0.25, 0.5, and so on, forever. Here is how we could use the generator:

```
result = []

for x in quarters():

    result.append(x)

    if x >= 1.0:

        break
```

The break command is useful - without that, the for ... in loop would never finish!

At the end the result list is [0.0, 0.25, 0.5, 0.75, 1.0].

Each time we call quarters() we get back a generator that starts at 0.0 and increments by 0.25; yet imagine a scenario in which we need to reset the generator's present value. It is possible to pass a value into a generator, as this new version of the generator function shows:

```
def quarters(next_quarter=0.0):

    while True:
```

```python
        received = (yield next_quarter)

        if received is None:

            next_quarter += 0.25

        else:

            next_quarter = received
```

The yield expression restores each an incentive to the caller in return. What's more, if the caller calls the generator's send() technique, the worth sent is gotten in the generator function as the consequence of the yield expression. Here is the way we can utilize the new generator function:

```python
result = []

generator = quarters()

while len(result) < 5:

    x = next(generator)

    if abs(x - 0.5) < sys.float_info.epsilon:

        x = generator.send(1.0)

    result.append(x)
```

We make a variable to allude to the generator and call the implicit next() function which recovers the next thing from the generator it is given. (A similar impact can be accomplished by calling the generator's __next__() unique strategy, for this situation, x

= generator.__next__().) If the worth is equivalent to 0.5 we send the worth 1.0 into the generator (which quickly yields this value back). This time the outcome rundown is [0.0, 0.25, 1.0, 1.25, 1.5].

In the following subsection we will audit the enchantment numbers.py program which procedures files given on the command line. Sadly, the Windows shell ace gram (cmd.exe) doesn't give trump card development (likewise called file globing), so if a program is kept running on Windows with the contention *.*, the strict content "*.*" will go into the sys.argv list instead of the considerable number of files in the present directory. We tackle this issue by making two distinctive get_files() capacities, one for Windows and the other for Unix, the two of which use generators. Here's the code:

```
if sys.platform.startswith("win"):

    def get_files(names):

        for name in names:

            if os.path.isfile(name):

                yield name

            else:

                for file in glob.iglob(name):

                    if not os.path.isfile(file):

                        continue

                    yield file

else:

    def get_files(names):
```

112

```python
return (file for file in names if os.path.isfile(file))
```

In either case the function is relied upon to be called with a rundown of filenames, for instance, sys.argv[1:], as its contention.

On Windows the function repeats over every one of the names recorded. For every filename, the function yields the name, however for nonfiles (typically indexes), the glob module's glob.iglob() function is utilized to restore an iterator to the names of the files that the name speaks to after trump card extension. For a standard name like autoexec.bat an iterator that produces one thing (the name) is returned, and for a name that utilizations trump cards like *.txt an iterator that creates all the coordinating files (for this situation those with expansion .txt) is returned. (There is likewise a glob.glob() function that profits a rundown as opposed to an iterator.)

On Linux the shell does special case development for us, so we simply need to restore a generator for every one of the files whose names we have been given.

Generator functions can likewise be utilized as co-routines, on the off chance that we structure them effectively. Co-routines are functions that can be suspended in mid-execution (at the yield articulation), trusting that the yield will give an outcome to take a shot at, and once got they keep processing.

Chapter 2: Dynamic Code Execution

In some cases it is easier to write a bit of code that generates the code we need than to compose the required code legitimately. What's more, in some contexts it is useful to give users a chance to input code (for example, functions in a spreadsheet), and to give Python a chance to execute the entered code for us as opposed to compose a parser and handle it ourselves—in spite of the fact that executing self-assertive code like that may be a potential security risk, obviously. Another case that may need dynamic code execution is to give plug-ins to broaden a program's usefulness. Using these plugins has one significant disadvantage: all the necessary usefulness is not incorporated with the expert gram (which can make the program increasingly hard to convey and runs the risk of plug-ins getting lost), however the advantages has that plug-ins can be redesigned exclusively and can be given separately, perhaps to give enhancements that were not initially envisaged.

Dynamic Code Execution

The easiest way to execute an expression is to use the built-in eval() function. For example:

```
x = eval("(2 ** 31) - 1")          # x == 2147483647
```

This is fine for user-entered expressions, yet consider the possibility that we have to make a function progressively. For that we can utilize the inherent executive() function. For instance, the user might give us a formula such as $4\pi r^2$ and the name "area of sphere", which they want turned into a function. Assuming that x will be replaced with math..pi, the function they want can be created like this:

```python
import math

code = '''

def area_of_sphere(r):

    return 4 * math.pi * r ** 2

'''

context = {}

context["math"] = math

exec(code, context)
```

We should utilize appropriate space—all things considered, the cited code is standard Python. (In spite of the fact that for this situation we could have composed everything on a single line in light of the fact that the suite is only one line.)

On the off chance that exec() is called with some code as its solitary contention there is no real way to get to any functions or factors that are made because of the code being executed. Moreover, exec() can't get to any imported modules or any of the factors, functions, or different objects that are in degree at the purpose of the call. Both of these issues can be understood by passing a dictionary as the subsequent contention. The dictionary gives a spot where object references can be kept for getting to after the exec() call has wrapped up. For instance, the utilization of the setting dictionary implies that after the exec() call, the dictionary has an object reference to the area_of_sphere() function that was made by exec(). In this model we required exec() to have the option to get to the math module, so we embedded a thing into the setting dictionary whose key is the module's name and whose worth is an object reference to the comparing module object. This guarantees inside the exec() call, math.pi is open

.

Now and again it is advantageous to give the whole worldwide setting to exec(). This should be possible by passing the dictionary returned by the globals() function. One weakness of this methodology is that any objects made in the exec() call would be added to the worldwide dictionary. An answer is to duplicate the worldwide setting into a dictionary, for instance, setting = globals().copy(). This still gives exec() access to imported modules and the factors and different objects that are in scope, and in light of the fact that we have duplicated, any progressions to the setting made inside the exec() call are kept in the setting dictionary and are not spread to the worldwide condition. (It may have the earmarks of being progressively secure to utilize copy.deepcopy(), yet on the off chance that security is a worry it is ideal to keep away from exec() out and out.) We can likewise pass the local setting, for instance, by passing locals() as a third contention—this makes objects in the local scope accessible to the code executed by exec().

After the exec() call the context dictionary contains a key called "area_of_sphere" whose value is the area_of_sphere() function. Here is how we canaccess and call the function:

    area_of_sphere = context["area_of_sphere"]

    area = area_of_sphere(5)   # area == 314.15926535897933

The area_of_sphere object is an object reference to the function we have progressively made and can be utilized simply like some other function. Also, in spite of the fact that we made just a single function in the exec() call, not at all like eval(), which can work on just a single articulation, exec() can deal with the same number of Python proclamations as we like, including whole modules, as we will find in the following subsection.

Dynamically Importing Modules

Python gives three simple mechanisms that can be utilized to make plug-ins, all of which include bringing in modules by name at runtime. What's more, when we have powerfully imported extra modules, we can utilize Python's reflection functions to check the accessibility of the functionality we need, and to access it as required.

In this subsection we will survey the enchantment numbers.py program. This program peruses the initial 1 000 bytes of each record given on the command line and for every one outputs the document's sort (or the content "Obscure"), and the filename. Here is a model command line and a concentrate from its yield:

C:\Python31\python.exe magic-numbers.py c:\windows*.*

...

XML.................c:\windows\WindowsShell.Manifest

Unknown.............c:\windows\WindowsUpdate.log

Windows Executable..c:\windows\winhelp.exe

Windows Executable..c:\windows\winhlp32.exe

Windows BMP Image...c:\windows\winnt.bmp

...

The program tries to load in any module that is in the same catalog as the program and whose name contains the content "enchantment". Such modules are required to give a single open capacity, get_file_type(). Two exceptionally simple model modules, StandardMagicNumbers.py and WindowsMagicNumbers.py, that each have a get_file_type() functions are given the book's examples.

We will audit the program's fundamental() work in two parts.

```
def main():

    modules = load_modules()

    get_file_type_functions = []

    for module in modules:
```

```python
            get_file_type = get_function(module, "get_file_type")

        if get_file_type is not None:

            get_file_type_functions.append(get_file_type)
```

In a minute, we will take a gander at three distinct usage of the load_modules() function which returns a (potentially unfilled) rundown of module objects,and we will take a gander at the get_function() function further on. For every module discovered we attempt to recover a get_file_type() function, and add any we get to a rundown of such functions.

```python
for file in get_files(sys.argv[1:]):

    fh = None

    try:

        fh = open(file, "rb")

        magic = fh.read(1000)

        for get_file_type in get_file_type_functions:

            filetype = get_file_type(magic,

                                     os.path.splitext(file)[1])

            if filetype is not None: print("{0:.<20}{1}".format(filetype,
                file)) break

        else:
```

```python
        print("{0:.<20}{1}".format("Unknown", file))

    except EnvironmentError as err:

        print(err)

    finally:

        if fh is not None:

            fh.close()
```

This loop iterates over each file listed on the command line and for every one reads its first 1 000 bytes. It at that point tries each get_file_type() function thusly to see whether it can decide the present file's sort. On the off chance that the file type is stop mined, the details are printed and the inward loop is broken out of, with processing proceeding with the following file. In the event that no function can decide the file type—or if no get_file_type() functions were discovered—an "unknown" line is printed.

We will currently survey three unique (however proportionate) methods for progressively bringing in modules, beginning with the longest and most troublesome methodology, since it demonstrates each progression expressly:

```python
def load_modules():

    modules = []

    for name in os.listdir(os.path.dirname(__file__) or "."):

        if name.endswith(".py") and "magic" in name.lower():

            filename = name
```

120

```python
        name = os.path.splitext(name)[0]

    if name.isidentifier() and name not in sys.modules:
```

```python
        fh = None

        try:

                fh = open(filename, "r", encoding="utf8")

                code = fh.read()

                module = type(sys)(name)

                sys.modules[name] = module

                exec(code, module.__dict__)

                modules.append(module)

        except (EnvironmentError, SyntaxError) as err:

                sys.modules.pop(name, None)

                print(err)

        finally:

                if fh is not None:

                        fh.close()

        return modules
```

We start by emphasizing over every one of the documents in the program's index. On the off chance that this is the present registry, os.path.dirname(__file__) will restore an unfilled string which would cause os.listdir() to raise a special case, so we pass "." if important. For every competitor document (closes with .py and contains the content "enchantment"), we get the module name by cleaving off the record extension. On the off chance that the name is a legitimate identifier it is a suitable module name, and in the event that it isn't as of now in the worldwide rundown of modules kept up in the sys.modules dictionary we can attempt to import it.

We read the content of the record into the code string. The following line, module =type(sys)(name), is very inconspicuous. When we call type() it restores the sort objectof the object it is given. So on the off chance that we called type(1) we would get int back. On the off chance that we print the sort object we simply get something intelligible like "int", yet on the off chance that we call the sort object as a capacity, we recover an object of that type. For instance, we can get the integer 5 in variable x by composing x = 5, or x = int(5), or x = type(0)(5), or int_type = type(0); x = int_type(5). For this situation we've utilized type(sys) and sys is a module, so we get back the module type object (basically equivalent to a class object), and can utilize it to make another module with the given name. Similarly as with the int model where it didn't make a difference what integer we used to get the int type object, it doesn't make a difference what module we use (as long as it is one that exists, that is, has been imported) to get the module type object.

When we have another (vacant) module, we add it to the global list of modules to keep the module from being inadvertently reimported. This is done before calling exec() to all the more closely mirror the conduct of the import statement. At that point we call exec() to execute the code we have perused—and we use the module's word reference as the code's unique situation. Toward the end we add the module to the list of modules we will pass back. Furthermore, if an issue arises, we erase the module from the global modules word reference in the event that it has been included—it won't have been added to the list of modules if an error happened. Notice that exec() can deal with any

Syntax	Description
__import__(...)	Imports a module by name; see text
compile(source, file, mode)	Returns the code object that results from compiling the source text; file should be the filename, or "<string>"; mode must be "single", "eval", or "exec"
delattr(obj, name)	Deletes the attribute called name from object obj
dir(*obj*)	Returns the list of names in the local scope, or if *obj* is given then *obj*'s names (e.g., its attributes and methods)
eval(source, *globals*, *locals*)	Returns the result of evaluating the single expression in source; if supplied,*globals*is the global context and*locals* is the local context (as dictionaries)
exec(obj, *globals*, *locals*)	Evaluates object obj, which can be a string or a code object from compile(), and returns None; if supplied, *globals* is the global context and *locals* is the local context
getattr(obj, name, *val*)	Returns the value of the attribute called name from object obj, or*val*if given and there is no such attribute
globals()	Returns a dictionary of the current global context

hasattr(obj, name)	Returns True if object obj has an attribute called name
locals()	Returns a dictionary of the current local context
setattr(obj, name, val)	Sets the attribute called name to the value val for the object obj, creating the attribute if necessary
type(obj)	Returns object obj's type object
vars(obj)	Returns object obj's context as a dictionary; or the local context if obj is not given

quantity of code (where eval() evaluates an expression—see Table 8.1), and may raise a SyntaxError exception.

Here's the second way to dynamically load a module at runtime—the code shown here replaces the first approach's try ... except block:

```
try:

    exec("import " + name)

    modules.append(sys.modules[name])

except SyntaxError as err:

    print(err)
```

One hypothetical issue with this methodology is that it is conceivably uncertain. The name variable could start with sys; and be trailed by some ruinous code.

What's more, here is the third approach, again simply demonstrating the replacement for the principal approach's attempt ... aside from block:

```
try:

    module = __import__(name)

    modules.append(module)

except (ImportError, SyntaxError) as err:

    print(err)
```

This is the most simple way to deal with capably import modules and is fairly more secure than using executive(), though like any one of a kind import, it is by no means, secure in light of the fact that we haven't the foggiest what is being executed when the module is imported.

None of the systems showed up here handles packs or modules in different ways, yet it isn't difficult to loosen up the code to suit these—disregarding the way that it justifies examining the online documentation, especially for __import__(), if greater advancement is required.

Having imported the module we ought to have the alternative to get to the value it gives. This can be cultivated utilizing Python's worked in introspection functions, getattr() and hasattr(). Here's the methods by which we have used them to realize the get_function() work:

```
def get_function(module, function_name):
```

126

```python
    function = get_function.cache.get((module, function_name), None)

    if function is None:

        try:

            function = getattr(module, function_name)

            if not hasattr(function, "__call__"):

                raise AttributeError()

            get_function.cache[module, function_name] = function

        except AttributeError:

            function = None

    return function

get_function.cache = {}
```

Overlooking the reserve related code for a minute, what the function does is call getattr() on the module object with the name of the function we need. Ifthere is no such property an AttributeError special case is raised, yet in the event that there is such a trait we use hasattr() to watch that the quality itself has the __call__ characteristic—something that all callables (functions and methods) have.
(Further on we will see a more pleasant method for checking whether a characteristic is callable.) If the trait exists and is callable we can return it to the caller; else, we return None to connote that the function isn't accessible.
In the event that several records were being processed (e.g., because of utilizing *.* in the C:\windows index), we would prefer not to experience the query procedure for each module for each document. So following

127

characterizing the get_function() function, we add an ascribe to the function, a dictionary called cache. (When all is said in done, Python enables us to add self-assertive attributes to discretionary articles.) The first occasion when that get_function() is known as the cache dictionary is unfilled, so the dict.get() call will return None. In any case, each time an appropriate function is discovered it is placed in the dictionary with a 2-tuple of the module and function name utilized as the key and the function itself as the worth. So the second and every single resulting time a specific function is mentioned the function is quickly come back from the cache and no quality query happens by any stretch of the imagination

The method utilized for storing the get_function's() arrival esteem for a given arrangement of contentions is called retaining. It tends to be utilized for any function that has no symptoms (doesn't change any worldwide variables), and that consistently restores a similar outcome for the equivalent (unchanging) contentions. Since the code required to make and deal with a cache for each remembered function is the equivalent, it is an ide-al contender for a function decorator, and a few @memorize decorator plans are given in the Python Cookbook, in code.activestate.com/plans/langs/python/. Notwithstanding, module items are alterable, so some off-the-rack retained decorators wouldn't work with our get_function() function the way things are. A simple arrangement is utilize every module's __name__ string as opposed to the module itself as the initial segment of the key tuple.

Doing dynamic module imports is simple, as is executing self-assertive Python code utilizing the executive() function. This can be extremely helpful, for instance, enabling us to store code in a database. Notwithstanding, we have no influence over what imported or executed code will do. Review that notwithstanding variables, functions, and classes, modules can likewise contain code that is executed when it is imported—if the code originated from an un-confided in source it may accomplish something horrendous. The most effective method to address this relies upon conditions, in spite of the fact that it may not be an issue at all in certain situations, or for individual projects.

Function and Method Decorators

A decorator is a kind of function that can accept a function or technique as its sole contention and returns another function or strategy that fuses the finished function or strategy with some extra functionality included. We have just utilized some predefined decorators, for instance, @property and @classmethod. In this subsection we will figure out how to make our own function decorators, and later in this section we will perceive how to make class decorators.

For our first decorator model, let us guess that we have numerous functions that perform figurings, and that a portion of these must consistently deliver a positive outcome. We could add a statement to each of these, however utilizing a decorator is simpler and more clear. Here's a function beautified with the @positive_result decorator that we will make in a minute:

```
@positive_result

def discriminant(a, b, c):

    return (b ** 2) - (4 * a * c)
```

On account of the decorator, if the outcome is ever under 0, an Assertion Error special case will be raised and the program will end. What's more, obviously, we can utilize the decorator on the same number of functions as we like. Here's the decorator's usage:

```
def positive_result(function):

    def wrapper(*args, **kwargs):

        result = function(*args, **kwargs)

        assert result >= 0, function.__name__ + "() result isn't >= 0" return result

    wrapper.__name__ = function.__name__

    wrapper.__doc__ = function.__doc__
```

```
        return wrapper
```

Decorators characterize another neighborhood function that calls the first function. Here, the neighborhood function is wrapper(); it considers the first function and stores the outcome, and it utilizes an affirmation to ensure that the outcome is certain (or that the program will end). The wrapper wraps up by restoring the outcome computed by the wrapped function. In the wake of making the wrapper, we set its name and doc-string to those of the first function. This assists with reflection, since we need mistake messages to specify the name of the first function, not the wrapper. At last, we return the wrapper function—it is this function will be utilized instead of the first.

```
    def positive_result(function):

        @functools.wraps(function)

        def wrapper(*args, **kwargs):

            result = function(*args, **kwargs)

            assert result >= 0, function.__name__ + "() result isn't >= 0" return result


        return wrapper
```

Here is a marginally cleaner variant of the @positive_result decorator. The wrap-per itself is wrapped utilizing the functools module's @functools.wraps decorator, which guarantees that the wrapper() function has the name and doc-string of the first function.

Now and again it is helpful to have the option to parameterize a decorator, however from the start locate this doesn't appear to be conceivable since a decorator takes only one contention, a function or technique. Be that as it may, there's a perfect answer for this. We can call a function with the parameters we need and that profits a decorator which would then be able to enrich the function that tails it. For instance:

```python
@bounded(0, 100)

def percent(amount, total):

    return (amount / total) * 100
```

Here, the bounded() function is called with two contentions, and returns a decorator that is utilized to design the percent() function. The motivation behind the decorator for this situation is to ensure that the number returned is consistently in the range 0 to 100 comprehensive. Here's the execution of the bounded() function:

```python
def bounded(minimum, maximum):

    def decorator(function):

        @functools.wraps(function)

        def wrapper(*args, **kwargs):

            result = function(*args, **kwargs)

            if result < minimum:

                return minimum
```

```
        elif result > maximum:

            return maximum

        return result

    return wrapper

    return decorator
```

The function makes a decorator function, that itself makes a wrapper function. The wrapper performs the calculation and returns an outcome that is inside the limited range. The decorator() function restores the wrapper() function, and the limited function restores the decorator.

One further point to note is that each time a wrapper is made inside the limited function, the specific wrapper utilizes the base and most extreme values that were passed to limited.

The last decorator we will make in this subsection is more mind boggling. It is a logging function that records the name, contentions, and aftereffect of any function it is utilized to decorate. For instance:

```
@logged

def discounted_price(price, percentage, make_integer=False):

    result = price * ((100 - percentage) / 100)

    if not (0 < result <= price):

        raise ValueError("invalid price")
```

```python
return result if not make_integer else int(round(result))
```

In the event that Python is kept running in debug mode (the ordinary mode), each time the limited value function is known as a log message will be added to the document logged.log in the machine's local brief index, as this log record extract illustrates:

called: discounted_price(100, 10) -> 90.0

called: discounted_price(210, 5) -> 199.5

called: discounted_price(210, 5, make_integer=True) -> 200

called: discounted_price(210, 14, True) -> 181

called: discounted_price(210, -8) <type 'ValueError'>: invalid price

In the event that Python is kept running in improved mode (utilizing the - O command-line alternative or in the event that the PYTHONOPTIMIZE condition variable is set to - O), at that point no logging will happen. Here's the code for starting logging and for the decorator:

```
if __debug__:

    logger = logging.getLogger("Logger")

    logger.setLevel(logging.DEBUG)

    handler = logging.FileHandler(os.path.join( tempfile.gettempdir(), "logged.log"))
    logger.addHandler(handler)


    def logged(function):

        @functools.wraps(function)
```

```python
def wrapper(*args, **kwargs):

    log = "called: " + function.__name__ + "("

    log += ", ".join(["{0!r}".format(a) for a in args] +
                      ["{0!s}={1!r}".format(k, v)

                       for k, v in kwargs.items()])

    result = exception = None

    try:

        result = function(*args, **kwargs)

        return result

    except Exception as err:

        exception = err

    finally:

        log += ((") -> " + str(result)) if exception is None else ") {0}: \
                {1}".format(type(exception),

                            exception))

        logger.debug(log)

        if exception is not None:

            raise exception

return wrapper
```

```python
else:

    def logged(function):

        return function
```

In debug mode the worldwide variable __debug__ is True. If so we set up logging using the logging module, and after that make the @logged decorator. The logging module is exceptionally incredible and adaptable—it can log to files, pivoted files, emails, network connections, HTTP servers, and that's just the beginning. Here we've used just the most basic facilities by making a logging object, setting its logging level (several levels are supported), and choosing to use a document for the output.

The wrapper's code begins by setting up the log string with the function's name and arguments. We at that point take a stab at calling the function and storing its result. On the off chance that any exemption occurs we store it. In all cases the at long last square is executed, and there we include the arrival worth (or special case) to the log string and keep in touch with the log. On the off chance that no exemption happened, the result is returned; otherwise, we re-raise the special case to accurately mimic the first function's conduct.

In the event that Python is running in optimized mode, __debug__ is False; in this case we characterize the logged() function to simply restore the function it is given, so separated from the small overhead of this indirection when the function is first made, there is no runtime overhead by any means.

Note that the standard library's follow and cProfile modules can run and examine programs and modules to deliver various following and profiling reports. Both use introspection, so dissimilar to the @logged decorator we have used here, neither follow nor cProfile requires any source code changes.

Function Annotations

Functions and methods can be characterized with annotations—expressions that can be used in a function's signature. Here's the general syntax:

def *functionName*(*par1* : *exp1*, *par2* : *exp2*, ..., *parN* : *expN*) ->*rexp*:

   suite

137

Each colon articulation part (:expX) is a discretionary explanation, as is the bolt return articulation part (- >rexp). The last (or just) positional parameter (if present) can be of the structure *args, with or without an explanation; comparably, the last (or just) keyword parameter (if present) can be of the structure **kwargs, again with or without a comment.

In the event that annotations are available they are added to the capacity's __annotations__ dictionary; in the event that they are absent this dictionary is vacant. The dictionary's keys are the parameter names, and the qualities are the relating expressions. The syntax enables us to annotate all, a few, or none of the parameters and to annotate the arrival esteem or not. Annotations have no exceptional centrality to Python. The main thing that Python does even with annotations is to placed them in the __annotations__ dictionary; some other action is up to us. Here is a case of an annotated capacity that is in the Util module:

```python
def is_unicode_punctuation(s : str) -> bool:

    for c in s:

        if unicodedata.category(c)[0] != "P":

            return False

    return True
```

Each Unicode character has a place with a specific classification and every class is distinguished by a two-character identifier. Every one of the classes that start with P are punctuation characters.

Here we have utilized Python information types as the annotation expressions. Be that as it may, they have no specific importance for Python, as these calls should clarify:

```python
Util.is_unicode_punctuation("zebr\a")
                                        # returns: False

Util.is_unicode_punctuation(s="!@#?")
                                        # returns: True

Util.is_unicode_punctuation(("!", "@"))
                                        # returns: True
```

The main call utilizes a positional contention and the second call a catchphrase contention, just to demonstrate that the two sorts fill in true to form. The last call passes a tuple instead of a string, and this is acknowledged since Python does just record the annotations in the __annotations__ dictionary.

In the event that we need to offer importance to annotations, for instance, to give type checking, one methodology is to design the capacities we need the significance to apply to with a reasonable decorator. Here is a fundamental kind checking decorator:

```python
def strictly_typed(function):

    annotations = function.__annotations__

    arg_spec = inspect.getfullargspec(function)

    assert "return" in annotations, "missing type for return value"

    for arg in arg_spec.args + arg_spec.kwonlyargs:

        assert arg in annotations, ("missing type for parameter '" + arg + "'")


    @functools.wraps(function)

    def wrapper(*args, **kwargs):

        for name, arg in (list(zip(arg_spec.args, args)) +
                          list(kwargs.items())):
            assert isinstance(arg, annotations[name]), (

                "expected argument '{0}' of {1} got {2}".format(

                name, annotations[name], type(arg)))

        result = function(*args, **kwargs)

        assert isinstance(result, annotations["return"]), ( "expected return of
                {0} got {1}".format( annotations["return"],
                type(result)))
```

```
        return result

    return wrapper
```

This decorator necessitates that each contention and the arrival value must be annotated with the normal sort. It watches that the function's contentions and return type are altogether annotated with their sorts when the function it is passed is made, and at runtime it watches that the kinds of the real contentions coordinate those normal.

The assess module gives ground-breaking introspection administrations to objects. Here, we have utilized just a little piece of the contention detail object it returns, to get the names of each positional and keyword contention—in the right request on account of the positional contentions. These names are then utilized related to the annotations word reference to guarantee that each parameter and the arrival value are annotated.

The wrapper function made inside the decorator starts by repeating over each name–contention pair of the given positional and keyword contentions. Since zip() restores an iterator and dictionary.items() restores a word reference see we can't link them legitimately, so first we convert them both to records. On the off chance that any genuine contention has an alternate sort from its comparing annotation the statement will fall flat; generally, the real function is called and the kind of the value returned is checked, and on the off chance that it is of the correct kind, it is returned. Toward the finish of the strictly_typed() function, we return the wrapped function of course. Notice that the checking is done uniquely in debug mode (which is Python's default mode—constrained by the - O command-line choice and the PYTHONOPTIMIZE condition variable).

On the off chance that we enhance the is_unicode_punctuation() function with the @strictly_typed decorator, and attempt indistinguishable models from before utilizing the adorned form, the annotations are followed up on:

is_unicode_punctuation("zebr\a")
                                                    # returns: False

is_unicode_punctuation(s="!@#?")
                                                    # returns: True

is_unicode_punctuation(("!", "@"))

142

```
# raises AssertionError
```

Presently the contention types are checked, so in the last case an Assertion Error is raised on the grounds that a tuple isn't a string or a subclass of str.

Presently we will take a gander at a totally extraordinary utilization of annotations. Here's a little function that has a similar functionality as the inherent range() function, then again, actually it generally returns coasts:

```
def range_of_floats(*args) -> "author=Reginald Perrin":

    return (float(x) for x in range(*args))
```

No utilization is made of the explanation by the capacity itself, however it is anything but difficult to envisage a tool that imported the majority of an undertaking's modules and created a rundown of capacity names and creator names, extracting each capacity's name from its __name__ attribute, and the creator names from the value of the __annotations__ word reference's "return" item.

Chapter 3: Further Object-Oriented Programming

Annotations are another feature of Python, and on the grounds that Python doesn't force any predefined importance on them, the utilizations they can be put to are constrained distinctly by our creative mind.

In this section we will look all the more profoundly into Python's help for item direction, learning numerous strategies that can diminish the measure of code we should compose, and that extend the power and abilities of the programming highlights that are accessible to us. In any case, we will start with one little and basic new element. Here is the beginning of the meaning of a Point class.

```python
class Point:

    __slots__ = ("x", "y")

    def __init__(self, x=0, y=0):

        self.x = x

        self.y = y
```

At the point when a class is made without the utilization of __slots__, in the background Python makes a private dictionary called __dict__ for each occasion, and this dictionary holds the case's information attributes. This is the reason we can include or re-move attributes from objects.

On the off chance that we just need objects where we get to the first attributes and don't have to include or evacuate attributes, we can make classes that don't have a __dict__. This is accomplished basically by characterizing a class attribute called __slots__ whose worth is a tuple of attribute names. Each object of such a class will have attributes of the predetermined names and no __dict__; no attributes can be included or expelled from such classes. These objects devour less memory and are quicker than customary objects, despite the fact that this is probably not going to have a lot of effect except if huge quantities of objects are made. On the off chance that we acquire from a class that utilizations __slots__ wemustdeclare slots in our subclass, regardless of whether vacant, for example, __slots__

145

= the memory and speed reserve funds will be lost.

(); or ## Controlling Attribute Access

It is once in a while advantageous to have a class where attribute esteems are computed on the fly as opposed to stored. Here's the finished usage of such a class:

```
class Ord:

    def __getattr__(self, char):

        return ord(char)
```

With the Ord class accessible, we can make an occurrence, ord = Ord(), and afterward have an option to the worked in ord() function that works for any character that is a valid identifier. For instance, ord.a returns 97, ord.Z returns 90, and ord.å returns 229. (Be that as it may, ord.! furthermore, comparable are syntax blunders.)

Note that in the event that we composed the Ord class into IDLE it would not work on the off chance that we, at that point composed ord = Ord(). This is on the grounds that the example has a similar name as the inherent ord() function that the Ord class utilizes, so the ord() call would really turn into a call to the ord occasion and result in a TypeError special case. The issue would not emerge on the off chance that we imported a module containing the Ord class on the grounds that the intuitively made ord object and the inherent ord() function utilized by the Ord class would be in two separate modules, so one would not dislodge the other. In the event that we truly need to make a class intuitively and to reuse the name of an inherent we can do as such by guaranteeing that the class calls the implicit—for this situation by bringing in the builtins module which gives unambiguous access to all the inherent functions, and calling builtins.ord() as opposed to plain ord().

Here's another small yet complete class. This one enables us to make "constants". It isn't hard to change the values despite the class' good faith, however it can in any event anticipate basic errors.

```
class Const:

    def __setattr__(self, name, value):
```

147

```python
        if name in self.__dict__:

            raise ValueError("cannot change a const attribute")

        self.__dict__[name] = value


    def __delattr__(self, name):

        if name in self.__dict__:

            raise ValueError("cannot delete a const attribute") raise
AttributeError("'{0}' object has no attribute '{1}'"

                .format(self.__class__.__name__, name))
```

With this class we can make a steady article, say, const = Const(), and set any attributes we like on it, for instance, const.limit = 591. However, when a quality's value has been set, despite the fact that it very well may be perused as regularly as we like, any endeavor to change or erase it will bring about a Value Error exemption being raised. We have not reimplemented __getattr__() in light of the fact that the base class object.__getattr__() strategy does what we need—restores the given quality's value or raises an AttributeError exemption if there is no such property. In the __delattr__() method we mimic the __getattr__() method's error message for nonexistent attributes, and to do this we must get the name of the class we are in as well as

148

Special Method	Usage	Description
__delattr__(self, name)	del x.n	Deletes object x's n attribute
__dir__(self)	dir(x)	Returns a list of x's attribute names
__getattr__(self, name)	v = x.n	Returns the value of object x's n attribute if it isn't found directly
__getattribute__(self, name)	v = x.n	Returns the value of object x's n attribute; see text
__setattr__(self, name, value)	x.n = v	Sets object x's n attribute's value to v

the name of the non-existent attribute.
This class works, because we are using the object's __dict__ property which is what its base class __getattr__(), __setattr__(), and __delattr__() methods use, even if, this time we have used only the base class's __getattr__().

There is another way of managing constants: we can also use named tuples. Here's a few examples:

Const = collections.namedtuple("_", "min max")(191, 591)

```python
Const.min, Const.max # returns: (191, 591)

Offset = collections.namedtuple("_", "id name description")(*range(3))

Offset.id, Offset.name, Offset.description # returns: (0, 1, 2)
```

In the two cases we have quite recently utilized a cast off name for the named tuple on the grounds that we need only one named tuple case each time, not a tuple subclass for making occurrences of a named tuple. In spite of the fact that Python doesn't bolster an enum information type, we can utilize tuples as we did now to get a similar result.

For our last see quality access exceptional strategies we will make an Image class whose width, height, and foundation shading are fixed when an Image is made (despite the fact that they are changed if an image is stacked). We gave access to them utilizing read-just properties. For instance, we had:

```python
@property

def width(self):

return self.__width
```

This is anything but difficult to code however could end up repetitive if there are a great deal of perused just properties. Here is an alternate arrangement that handles all the Image class' perused just properties in a single technique:

```python
def __getattr__(self, name):

if name == "colors":

return set(self.__colors)

classname = self.__class__.__name__

if name in frozenset({"background", "width", "height"}):
```

```python
return self.__dict__["_{classname}__{name}".format(
**locals())]
raise AttributeError("'{classname}' object has no "
"attribute '{name}'".format(**locals()))
```

In the event that we endeavor to get to an article's characteristic and the quality isn't discovered, Python will call the __getattr__() strategy (giving it is executed, and that we have not reimplemented __getattribute__()), with the name of the trait as a parameter. Executions of __getattr__() must raise an AttributeError special case on the off chance that they don't deal with the given trait.

For instance, on the off chance that we have the announcement image.colors, Python will search for a hues ascribe and having neglected to discover it, will at that point call Image.__getattr__(image, "hues"). For this situation the __getattr__() technique handles a "hues" attributename and restores a duplicate of the arrangement of hues that the picture is utilizing.

Different attributes are changeless, so they are sheltered to return straightforwardly to the guest. We could have composed separate elif articulations for every one like this:

```python
elif name == "background":
return self.__background
```

This time, anyway, we chose a compact way.
We know that, under the hood, every object's nonspecial attributes is held in self.__dict__, we chose to access them directly.
Also, remember that, for private attributes, the name is crippled to have the form _className__attributeName, so we must take this into account when getting the attribute's value from the object.

For the name mangling needed to look up private attributes and to provide the standard AttributeError error text, we need to know the name of the class we are in. (It may not be Image because the object might be an instance of an Image subclass.) Every object has a __class__ special attribute, so self.__class__ is always available inside methods and can safely be accessed by __getattr__() without risking unwanted recursion.

Note that there is a subtle difference in that using __getattr__() and self.__class__ provides access to the attribute in the instance's class (whichmay be a subclass), but accessing the attribute directly uses the class the at-tribute is defined in.

One extraordinary method that we have not secured is __getattribute__(). Where-as the __getattr__() method is called last when searching for (nonspecial) attributes, the __getattribute__() method is called first for each quality access. In spite of the fact that it tends to be valuable or even fundamental now and again to call __getattribute__(), reimplementing the __getattribute__() method can betricky. Reimplementations must be mindful so as not to call themselves recursively—utilizing super().__getattribute__() or object.__getattribute__() is frequently done in such cases. Likewise, since __getattribute__() is required each quality access, reimplementing it can without much of a stretch wind up debasing execution contrasted and direct property access or properties. None of the classes introduced in this book reimplements the __getattribute__() function.

Functors

In Python a function object is an object reference to any callable, for example, a function, a lambda function, or a method. The definition likewise incorporates classes, since an object reference to a class is a callable that, when called, restores an object of the given class—for instance, x = int(5). In software engineering a functor is an object that can be called like a function. So, in Python, terms a functor is simply one more sort of function object. Any class that has a __call__() uncommon method is a functor. The key advantage that functors offer is that they can keep up some state data. For instance, we could make a functor that consistently takes essential punctuation from the parts of the bargains. We would make and utilize it like this:

strip_punctuation = Strip(",;:.!?")

strip_punctuation("Land ahoy!") # returns: 'Land ahoy'

Here we make an occurrence of the Strip functor instating it with the worth ",;:.!?". At whatever point the example is called it restores the string it is passed with any punctuation characters peeled off. Here's the finished execution of the Strip class:

```
class Strip:

def __init__(self, characters):

self.characters = characters

def __call__(self, string):

return string.strip(self.characters)
```

We could accomplish something very similar utilizing a plain function or lambda, yet on the off chance that we have to store a bit more state or perform increasingly complex processing, a functor is frequently the correct arrangement.

A functor's capacity to catch state by utilizing a class is adaptable and control ful, however once in a while it is more than we truly need. Another approach to catch state is to utilize a closure. A closure is a function or strategy that catches some outer state. For instance:

```
def make_strip_function(characters):

def strip_function(string):

return string.strip(characters)

return strip_function

strip_punctuation = make_strip_function(",;:.!?")

strip_punctuation("Land ahoy!") # returns: 'Land ahoy'
```

This make_strip_function() function takes the characters to be stripped as its sole contention and returns another function, strip_function(), that

153

takes a string contention and which strips the characters that were given at the time the conclusion was made. So similarly as we can make the same number of occasions of the Strip class as we need, each with its very own characters to strip, we can make the same number of strip functions with their very own characters as we like.

The great use case for functors is to give key functions to sort routines.

Here is a nonexclusive SortKey functor class (from document SortKey.py):

class SortKey:

def __init__(self, *attribute_names):

self.attribute_names = attribute_names

def __call__(self, instance):

values = []

for attribute_name in self.attribute_names:

values.append(getattr(instance, attribute_name))

return values

At the point when a SortKey object is made it keeps a tuple of the attribute names it was initialized with. At the point when the object is called it makes a rundown of the attribute values for the occasion it is passed—in the request they were indicated when the SortKey was initialized. For instance, envision we have a Person class:

class Person:

def __init__(self, forename, surname, email):

self.forename = forename

self.surname = surname

self.email = email

Assume we have a list of Person objects in the individuals list. We can now sort the list by surnames like this: people.sort(key=SortKey("surname")). On the off chance that there are many individuals there will undoubtedly be some surname conflicts, so we can sort by surname, and after that by forename inside surname, similar to this: peo-ple.sort(key=SortKey("surname", "forename")). Plus, on the off chance that we had individuals with thesame surname and forename we could include the email attribute as well. Furthermore, of

course, we could sort by forename and afterward surname by changing the request for the attribute names we provide for the SortKey functor.

Another method for accomplishing something very similar, yet without expecting to make a func-tor by any stretch of the imagination, is to utilize the administrator module's operator.attrgetter() function. For instance, to sort by surname we could compose: people.sort(key=operator.attr-getter("surname")). Furthermore, correspondingly, to sort by surname and forename: people.sort(key=operator.attrgetter("surname", "forename")). The administrator. attrgetter() function restores a function (a conclusion) that, when approached an ob-ject, restores those attributes of the object that were indicated when the conclusion was made.

Functors are most likely utilized preferably less every now and again in Python over in different dialects that help them since Python has different methods for doing likewise things—for instance, utilizing terminations or thing and trait getters.

Context Managers

Setting managers enable us to streamline code by guaranteeing that specific show tions are performed when a specific square of code is executed. The conduct is accomplished in light of the fact that setting managers characterize two uncommon methods, __enter__() and __exit__(), that Python treats extraordinarily in the extent of a with explanation. At the point when a setting director is made in a with proclamation its __en-ter__() method is consequently called, and when

155

the setting administrator goes outof scope after its with explanation its __exit__() method is naturally called.

We can make our very own custom setting managers or use predefined ones—as we will see later in this subsection, the document articles returned by the implicit open() work are setting managers. The punctuation for utilizing setting managersis this:

with *expression* as *variable*:

suite

The articulation must be or should deliver a setting chief article; if the discretionary as factor part is determined, the variable is set to allude to the item returned by the setting administrator's __enter__() technique (and this is frequently the setting supervisor itself). Since a setting chief is ensured to execute its "leave" code (even despite exemptions), setting administrators can be utilized to take out the requirement for at last squares by and large.

A portion of Python's sorts are setting supervisors—for instance, all the file objects that open() can return—so we can dispense with at last squares when doing file taking care of as these comparable code snippets represent (expecting that procedure() is a capacity characterized somewhere else):

```
fh = None

try:

    fh = open(filename)

    for line in fh:

        process(line)

except EnvironmentError as err:

    print(err)

finally:

    if fh is not None:

        fh.close()
```

```
try:

    with open(filename) as fh:

        for line in fh:

            process(line)

except EnvironmentError as err:

    print(err)
```

A file item is a context supervisor whose leave code consistently shuts the file on the off chance that it was opened. The leave code is executed whether a special case happens, yet in the last case, the exemption is engendered. This guarantees the file gets shut despite everything we find the opportunity to deal with any errors, for this situation by printing a message for the client.

Truth be told, context administrators don't need to proliferate exemptions, however not doing so successfully shrouds any special cases, and this would more likely than not be a coding error. All the implicit and standard library context supervisors engender special cases.

Here and there we have to utilize more than one context chief simultaneously.

For instance:

```
try:

    with open(source) as fin:

        with open(target, "w") as fout:

            for line in fin:

                fout.write(process(line))

except EnvironmentError as err:

    print(err)
```

Here we read lines from the source file and compose processed variants of them to the objective file.

Utilizing settled with articulations can rapidly prompt a great deal of space. Luckily, the standard library's contextlib module gives some extra help to setting administrators, including the contextlib.nested() work which enables at least two setting directors to be taken care of in the equivalent with explanation as opposed to settling with proclamations. Here is a trade for the code just appeared, however precluding the greater part of the lines that are indistinguishable from previously:

```
try:

    with contextlib.nested(open(source), open(target, "w")) as ( fin, fout):
```

```
for line in fin:
```

It is just important to utilize contextlib.nested() for Python 3.0; from Python 3.1 this function is deplored on the grounds that Python 3.1 can deal with different setting administrators in a solitary with proclamation. Here is a similar model—again excluding superfluous lines—yet this time for Python 3.1:
try:

with open(source) as fin, open(target, "w") as fout:

for line in fin:

Utilizing this language structure keeps setting chiefs and the variables they are related with together, making the with explanation significantly more clear than if we somehow happened to settle them or to utilize contextlib.nested().

It isn't just record objects that are setting administrators. For instance, a few stringing related classes utilized for locking are setting directors. Setting chiefs can likewise be utilized with decimal.Decimal numbers; this is helpful on the off chance that we need to perform a few estimations with specific settings, (for example, a specific exactness) as a result.

If we need to make a custom setting director we should make a class that gives two methods: __enter__() and __exit__(). At whatever point a with proclamation is utilized on an occurrence of such a class, the __enter__() method is called and the arrival worth is utilized for the as variable (or discarded if there isn't one). At the point when control leaves the extent of the with articulation the __exit__() method is called (with subtleties of an exemption on the off chance that one has happened gone as contentions).

Assume we need to perform a few operations on a rundown in an atomic way—that is, we either need every one of the operations to be done or none of them so the resultant rundown is consistently in a known state. For instance, on the off chance that we have a rundown of integers and need to attach a whole number, erase a whole number, and change a few integers, all as a single activity, we could compose code this way:

160

```
try:

    with AtomicList(items) as atomic:

        atomic.append(58289)

        del atomic[3]

        atomic[8] = 81738

        atomic[index] = 38172

except (AttributeError, IndexError, ValueError) as err:

    print("no changes applied:", err)
```

If there's no exception, all operations are applied to the main list, but otherwise, no change is applied at all. Now let's get to the AtomicList context manager code:

```
class AtomicList:

    def __init__(self, alist, shallow_copy=True):

        self.original = alist

        self.shallow_copy = shallow_copy

    def __enter__(self):

        self.modified = (self.original[:] if self.shallow_copy else
        copy.deepcopy(self.original))
        return self.modified

    def __exit__(self, exc_type, exc_val, exc_tb):

        if exc_type is None:

            self.original[:] = self.modified
```

At the point when the AtomicList item is made we hold a reference to the first list and note whether shallow duplicating is to be utilized. (Shallow duplicating is fine for lists of numbers or strings; yet for lists that contain lists or different accumulations, shallow replicating isn't adequate.)

At that point, when the AtomicList setting director article is utilized in the with statement its __enter__() technique is called. Now we duplicate the first list and return the duplicate with the goal that every one of the progressions can be made on the duplicate.

When we arrive at the finish of the with statement's extension the __exit__() strategy is called. In the event that no special case happened the exc_type ("exemption type") will be None and we realize that we can securely supplant the first list's items with the items from the altered list. (We can't do self.original = self.modified in light of the fact that that would simply supplant one item reference with another and would not influence the first list by any means.) But on the off chance that a special case happened, we don't do anything to the first list and the adjusted list is disposed of.

The arrival value of __exit__() is utilized to demonstrate whether any special case that happened ought to be engendered. A True value implies that we have dealt with any exemption thus no spread ought to happen. Ordinarily we generally return False or something that assesses to False in a Boolean setting to permit any special case that struck spread. By not giving an express return value, our __exit__() returns None which assesses to False and accurately makes any special case engender.

Custom setting administrators are utilized in to guarantee that attachment associations and gzipped files are shut.

Descriptors

Descriptors are classes which give access control to the qualities of different classes. Any class that executes at least one of the descriptor exceptional methods, __get__(), __set__(), and __delete__(), is defined as a descriptor.

The understood property() and class Python procedure() limits are executed using descriptors. The way to understanding descriptors is that regardless of the way that we make a case of it, in a class as a class quality, Python accesses the descriptor through the class' events.

To make things obvious, how about we envision that we have a class whose examples hold a few strings. We need to get to the strings in the ordinary way, for instance, as a property, however we additionally need to get a XML-got away form of the strings at whatever point we need. One basic arrangement would be that at whatever point a string is set we quickly make a XML-got away duplicate. In the event that we had a huge number of strings and just at any point read the XML form of a couple of them, we would squander a great deal of handling and memory to no end. So we will make a descriptor that will give XML-got away strings on interest without putting away them. We will begin with the start of the user (proprietor) class, that is, the class that uses the descriptor:

class Product:

__slots__ = ("__name", "__description", "__price")

name_as_xml = XmlShadow("name")

description_as_xml = XmlShadow("description")

def __init__(self, name, description, price):

self.__name = name

self.description = description

self.price = price

The main code we have not demonstrated are the properties; the name is a perused just property and the portrayal and cost are lucid/writable properties, all set up in the typical way. (All the code is in the XmlShadow.py record.) We have utilized the __slots__ variable to guarantee that the class has no __dict__ and can store just the three indicated private attributes; this isn't identified with or fundamental for our utilization of descriptors.

Taking into account the name_as_xml and description_as_xml class attributes are set to be occurrences of the XmlShadow descriptor. Albeit no Product object has a name_as_xml attribute or a description_as_xml attribute, because of the descript or we can compose code this way (here citing from the module's documentation):

```
>>> product = Product("Chisel <3cm>", "Chisel & cap", 45.25)

>>> product.name, product.name_as_xml, product.description_as_xml
('Chisel <3cm>', 'Chisel &lt;3cm&gt;', 'Chisel &amp; cap')
```

This code works because when we try to access, for example, the name_as_xml attribute, Python finds that the Product class has a descriptor with that name, and uses the descriptor to see the attribute's value.

Here's the code for the XmlShadow class:

```
class XmlShadow:

def __init__(self, attribute_name):

self.attribute_name = attribute_name

def __get__(self, instance, owner=None):

return xml.sax.saxutils.escape(

getattr(instance, self.attribute_name))
```

At the point when the name_as_xml and description_as_xml items are made we pass the name of the Product class' relating attribute to the XmlShadow initializ-er so the descriptor realizes which attribute to chip away at. At that point, when the name_as_xml or description_as_xml attribute is looked into, Python calls the de-scriptor's __get__() strategy.

The self contention is the occurrence of the descrip-tor, the case contention is simply the Product example (i.e., the product's), and the proprietor contention is the owning class (Product for this situation). We utilize the getat-tr() function to recover the significant attribute from the product (in this casethe applicable property), and return a XML-got away form of it.

In the event that the utilization case was that solitary a little extent of the products were accessed for their XML strings, yet the strings were regularly long and similar ones were much of the time accessed, we could utilize a cache. For instance:

```
class CachedXmlShadow:

def __init__(self, attribute_name): self.attribute_name = attribute_name
self.cache = {}

def __get__(self, instance, owner=None): xml_text =
self.cache.get(id(instance)) if xml_text is not None:

return xml_text

return self.cache.setdefault(id(instance), xml.sax.saxutils.escape(
getattr(instance, self.attribute_name)))
```

We store the exceptional character of the case as the key as opposed to the occasion itself since dictionary keys must be hashable (which IDs are), however we would prefer not to force that as a prerequisite on classes that utilization the CachedXmlShad-ow descriptor. The key is essential since descriptors are made per classrather than per case. (The dict.setdefault() technique advantageously restores the value for the given key, or if no item with that key is available, makes another item with the given key and value and returns the value.)

Having seen descriptors used to produce information without fundamentally storing it, we will presently take a gander at a descriptor that can be utilized to store the majority of an object's attribute information, with the object not expecting to store anything itself. In the test ple, we will simply utilize a lexicon, however in an increasingly reasonable setting, the information may be stored in a document or a database. Here's the beginning of a changed variant of the Point class that utilizes the descriptor (from the ExternalStorage.py file):

```python
class Point:

    __slots__ = ()

    x = ExternalStorage("x")

    y = ExternalStorage("y")

    def __init__(self, x=0, y=0):

        self.x = x

        self.y = y
```

By setting __slots__ to a void tuple we guarantee that the class can't store any information attributes whatsoever. At the point when self.x is doled out to, Python finds that there is a descriptor with the name "x", thus utilizes the descriptor's __set__() method. The remainder of the class isn't appeared, yet is equivalent to the first Point class appeared in Chapter 6. Here is the finished External Storage descriptor class:

```python
class ExternalStorage:

    __slots__ = ("attribute_name",)

    __storage = {}

    def __init__(self, attribute_name):

        self.attribute_name = attribute_name

    def __set__(self, instance, value):

        self.__storage[id(instance), self.attribute_name] = value

    def __get__(self, instance, owner=None):

        if instance is None:
```

return self

return self.__storage[id(instance), self.attribute_name]

Every External Storage object has a solitary information attribute, attribute_name, which holds the name of the proprietor class' information attribute. At whatever point an attribute is set we store its incentive in the private class lexicon, __storage. Essentially, at whatever point an attribute is recovered we get it from the __storage word reference.

Similarly as with all descriptor strategies, self is the occurrence of the descriptor object and example is the self of the object that contains the descriptor, so here self is an External Storage object and occasion is a Point object.

Despite the fact that __storage is a class attribute, we can access it as self.__storage (similarly as we can call strategies utilizing self.method()), on the grounds that Python will search for it as an example attribute, and not discovering it will at that point search for it as a class attribute. The one (hypothetical) hindrance of this methodology is that on the off chance that we have a class attribute and a case attribute with a similar name, one would cover up the other. (On the off chance that this were extremely an issue we could generally allude to the class attribute utilizing the class, that is, ExternalStorage.__storage. Albeit hard-coding the class doesn't play well with subclassing as a rule, it doesn't generally make a difference for private attributes since Python name-ravages the class name into them in any case.)

The execution of the __get__() uncommon technique is marginally more modern than before in light of the fact that we give a methods by which the ExternalStorage occasion itself can be accessed. For instance, on the off chance that we have p = Point(3, 4), we can access the x-arrange with p.x, and we can access the ExternalStorage object that holds all the xs with Point.x.

To finish our inclusion of descriptors we will make the Property descriptor that impersonates the conduct of the implicit property() function, in any event for setters and getters. The code is in Property.py. Here is the finished NameAndExtension class that utilizes it:

167

```python
class NameAndExtension:

def __init__(self, name, extension):

self.__name = name

self.extension = extension


@Property

def name(self):

return self.__name



# Uses the custom Property descriptor



@Property

def extension(self):



# Uses the custom Property descriptor


 return self.__extension

@extension.setter # Uses the custom Property descriptor def
extension(self, extension):
self.__extension = extension
```

The usage is just the same as for the built-in @property decorator and for the *@propertyName*.setter decorator. Here is the start of the Property descriptor' simplementation:

```python
class Property:

    def __init__(self, getter, setter=None):

        self.__getter = getter

        self.__setter = setter

        self.__name__ = getter.__name__
```

The class' initializer takes a couple of functions as arguments. On the off chance that it is used as a decorator, it will get just the enlivened capacity and this becomes the getter, while the setter is set to None. We use the getter's name as the property's name. So for every property, we have a getter, possibly a setter, and a name.

```python
    def __get__(self, instance, owner=None):

        if instance is None:

            return self

        return self.__getter(instance)
```

At the point when a property is gotten to we return the consequence of calling the getter function where we have passed the occasion as its first parameter. From the start locate, self.__getter() resembles a strategy call, however it isn't. Truth be told, self.__getter is an attribute, one that happens to hold an object reference to a strategy that was passed in. So what happens is that first we recover the attribute (self.__getter), and afterward we call it as a function (). Also, in light of the fact that it is called as a function as opposed to as a strategy we should go in the applicable self object unequivocally ourselves. What's more, on account of a descriptor oneself object (from the class that is utilizing the descriptor) is called case (since self is the descriptor object). The equivalent applies to the __set__() strategy.

```python
    def __set__(self, instance, value):

        if self.__setter is None:
```

```python
raise AttributeError("'{0}' is read-only".format( self.__name__))
return self.__setter(instance, value)
```

If no setter has been specified, we raise an AttributeError; otherwise, we call the setter with the instance and the new value.

```python
def setter(self, setter):
```

```python
self.__setter = setter
```

```python
return self.__setter
```

This strategy is considered when the interpreter comes to, for instance, @extension.setter, with the capacity it improves as its setter contention. It stores the setter technique it has been given (which would now be able to be utilized in the __set__() strategy), and returns the setter, since decorators should restore the capacity or technique they enliven.

We have now taken a gander at three very various employments of descriptors. Descriptors are an amazing and adaptable element that can be utilized to do bunches of in the engine work while seeming, by all accounts, to be straightforward characteristics in their customer (user) class.

Class Decorators

Similarly as we can make decorators for functions and strategies, we can likewise make decorators for whole classes. Class decorators take a class object (the aftereffect of the class explanation), and should restore a class—regularly an adjusted form of the class they enrich. In this subsection we will contemplate two class decorators to perceive how they can be executed.

For instance, here are the way the SortedList.clear() and SortedList.pop() strategies were executed:

```
def clear(self):

    self.__list = []


def pop(self, index=-1):

    return self.__list.pop(index)
```

There is nothing we can do about the unmistakable() technique since there is no comparing strategy for the rundown type, yet for pop(), and the other six strategies that SortedList delegates, we can just consider the rundown class' relating method.This should be possible by utilizing the @delegate class decorator from the book's Util module. Here is the beginning of another version of the SortedList class:

```
@Util.delegate("__list", ("pop", "__delitem__", "__getitem__",

                "__iter__", "__reversed__", "__len__", "__str__"))

class SortedList:
```

The principal contention is the name of the ascribe to delegate to, and the subsequent contention is an arrangement of at least one methods that we need the representative() decorator to actualize for us with the goal that we don't need to take the necessary steps ourselves. The SortedList class in the SortedListDelegate.py record utilizes this methodology and along these lines doesn't have any code for the methods recorded, despite the fact that it completely bolsters them. Here is the class decorator that executes the methods:

```python
def delegate(attribute_name, method_names):

    def decorator(cls):

        nonlocal attribute_name

        if attribute_name.startswith("__"):

            attribute_name = "_" + cls.__name__ + attribute_name for name in method_names:

            setattr(cls, name, eval("lambda self, *a, **kw: " "self.{0}.{1}(*a, **kw)".format(attribute_name, name)))

        return cls

    return decorator
```

ator. The decorator itself takes a solitary contention, a class (similarly as a function decorator takes a solitary function or strategy as its contention).

We couldn't utilize a plain decorator since we need to pass contentions to the decorator, so we have rather made a function that takes our contentions and that profits a class decor

We should utilize non-local so the settled function utilizes the attribute_name from the external degree instead of endeavoring to utilize one from its own extension. Furthermore, we should have the option to address the attribute name if important to assess the name ruining of private attributes. The decorator's conduct is very straightforward: It repeats over all the strategy names that the representative() function has been given, and for every one makes another technique which it sets as an attribute on the class with the given strategy name.

We have utilized eval() to make every one of the designated methods since it tends to be utilized to execute a solitary explanation, and a lambda proclamation delivers a strategy or function. For instance, the code executed to deliver the pop() technique is:

```
lambda self, *a, **kw: self._SortedList__list.pop(*a, **kw)
```

We utilize the * and ** contention structures to take into consideration any contentions despite the fact that the methods being appointed to have explicit contention records. For instance, list.pop() acknowledges a solitary list position (or nothing, in which case it defaults to the last thing). This is alright in such a case that an inappropriate number or sorts of contentions are passed, the rundown technique that is called to take the necessary steps will raise a fitting special case.

The underneath normal decorator we will overview was furthermore used in Chapter 6. When we realized the FuzzyBool class we referenced that we had given quite recently the __lt__() and __eq__() extraordinary techniques (for < and ==), and had created the different assessment strategies thusly. What we didn't show was the got done with start of the class definition:

```
@Util.complete_comparisons

class FuzzyBool:
```

ation administrators by utilizing the accompanying logical equivalences:

The other four examination administrators were given by the complete_comparisons() class decorator. Given a class that characterizes only< (or<and ==), the decorator delivers the missing correl

$$x = y \Leftrightarrow \neg (x < y \lor y < x)$$

$$x \neq y \Leftrightarrow \neg (x = y)$$

$$x > y \Leftrightarrow y < x$$

$$x \leq y \Leftrightarrow \neg (y < x)$$

$$x \geq y \Leftrightarrow \neg (x < y)$$

If the class to be decorated has < and ==, the decorator will use them both, falling back to doing everything in terms of < if that is the only operator

176

supplied. (In fact, Python automatically produces > if < is supplied, != if == is supplied, and >= if <= is supplied, so it is sufficient to just implement the three operators <, <=, and == and to leave Python to infer the others. However, using the class decorator reduces the minimum that we must implement to just <. This is convenient, and also ensures that all the comparison operators use the same consistent logic.)

```
def complete_comparisons(cls):

    assert cls.__lt__ is not object.__lt__, (

        "{0} must define < and ideally ==".format(cls.__name__))

    if cls.__eq__ is object.__eq__:

        cls.__eq__ = lambda self, other: (not

            (cls.__lt__(self, other) or cls.__lt__(other, self))) cls.__ne__ =
lambda self, other: not cls.__eq__(self, other) cls.__gt__ = lambda self, other:
cls.__lt__(other, self) cls.__le__ = lambda self, other: not cls.__lt__(other, self)
cls.__ge__ = lambda self, other: not cls.__lt__(self, other) return cls
```

One issue that the decorator appearances is that class object from which each different class is eventually determined characterizes every one of the six examination administrators, all of which raise a TypeError special case whenever utilized. So we have to know whether < and

== have been reimplemented (and are in this manner usable). This should effortlessly be possible by looking at the applicable extraordinary techniques in the class being brightened with those in article.

In the event that the brightened class doesn't have a custom < the statement falls flat since that is the decorator's base prerequisite. What's more, if there is a custom == we use it; else, we make one. At that point the various techniques are made and the adorned class, presently with every one of the six examination strategies, is returned.

Utilizing class decorators is likely the least difficult and most direct method for evolving classes. Another methodology is to utilize metaclasses, a point we will cover later in this part.

Abstract Base Classes

An abstract base class (ABC) is a special class that can't be utilized to make objects. Rather, the reason classes is to characterize interfaces, that is, to in actuality list the techniques and properties that classes that acquire the abstract base class must give. This is helpful in light of the fact that we can utilize an abstract base class as a sort of guarantee—a guarantee that any inferred class will give the techniques and properties that the abstract base class indicates.

ABC	Inherits	API	Examples
Number	object		complex, decimal.Decimal, float, fractions.Fraction, int
Complex	Number	==, !=, +, -, *, /, abs(), bool(), complex(), conjugate(); also real and imag properties	complex, decimal.Decimal, float, fractions.Fraction, int
Real	Complex	<,<=, ==, !=,>=,>, +, -, *, /, //, %, abs(), bool(), complex(), conjugate(), divmod(), float(), math.ceil(), math.floor(), round(), int trunc(); also real and imag properties	decimal.Decimal, float, fractions.Fraction, int
Rational	Real	<,<=, ==, !=,>=,>, +, -, *, /, //, %, abs(), bool(), complex(), conjugate(), divmod(), float(), math.ceil(), math.floor(), round(),	fractions.Fraction, int

179

Integral	Rational		int
		trunc(); also real, imag, numerator, and denominator properties	
Integral	Rational	<,<=, ==, !=,>=,>, +, -, *, /, //, %,<<,>>, ~,&, ^, |, abs(), bool(), complex(), conjugate(), divmod(), float(), math.ceil(), math.floor(), pow(), round(), trunc(); also real, imag, numerator, and denominator properties	int

Abstract base classes will be classes that have in any event one abstract strategy or property. Abstract techniques can be characterized with no usage (i.e., their suite is pass, or in the event that we need to drive reimplementation in a subclass, raiseNotImplementedError()), or with a real (solid) execution that canbe conjured from subclasses, for instance, when there is a typical case. They can likewise have other cement (i.e., nonabstract) strategies and properties.

Classes that get from an ABC can be utilized to make occasions just on the off chance that they reimplement all the abstract strategies and abstract properties they have inherited. For those abstract techniques that have solid executions (regardless of whether it is just pass), the inferred class could essentially utilize super() to utilize the ABC's rendition.

Any solid strategies or properties are accessible through legacy obviously. All ABCs must have a metaclass of abc.ABCMeta (from the abc module), or from one of its subclasses. We spread metaclasses somewhat further on.

Python gives two gatherings of conceptual base classes, one in the accumulations module and the other in the numbers module. They enable us to pose inquiries about an item; for instance, given a variable x, we can see whether it is an arrangement utilizing isinstance(x, collections.MutableSequence) or whether it is an entire number utilizing isinstance(x, numbers.Integral). This is especially helpful in perspective on Python's dynamic composing where we don't really have the foggiest idea (or care) what an article's sort is, however need to know whether it bolsters the operations we need to apply to it. The numeric and accumulation ABCs are recorded in Tables 8.3 and 8.4. The other significant ABC is io.IOBase from which all the record and stream-taking care of classes determine.

To completely coordinate our very own custom numeric and accumulation classes we should make them fit in with the standard ABCs. For instance, the SortedList class is a succession, however the way things are, isinstance(L, collections.Sequence) returns False if L is a SortedList. One simple approach to fix this is to acquire the pertinent ABC:

```
class SortedList(collections.Sequence):
```

By making collections.Sequence the base class, the isinstance() test will presently return True. Besides, we will be required to execute __init__() (or __new__()), __getitem__(), and __len__() (which we do). The collec-tions.Sequence ABC additionally gives concrete (i.e., nonabstract) implementationsfor __contains__(), __iter__(), __reversed__(), check(), and record(). On account of SortedList, we reimplement them all, however we could have utilized the ABC ver-sions on the off chance that we needed to, just by not reimplementing them. We can't make SortedList a subclass of collections.MutableSequence despite the fact that the listis alterable on the grounds that SortedList doesn't have every one of the techniques that a collec-tions.MutableSequence must give, for example, __setitem__() and annex(). (Thecode for this SortedList is in SortedListAbc.py. We will see an option ap-proach to making a SortedList into a collections.Sequence in the Metaclasses subsection.)

Since we have perceived how to make a custom class fit in with the

181

standard ABCs, we will go to another utilization of ABCs: to give an interface guarantee to our very own custom classes. We will take a gander at three rather various guides to cover various parts of making and utilizing ABCs.We will start with a very simple example that shows how to handle read-able/writable properties. The class is used to represent domestic appliances. Every appliance that is created must have a read-only model string and a read-able/writable price. We also want to ensure that the ABC's __init__() is reim-plemented. Here's the ABC (from Appliance.py); we have not shown the import

ABC	Inherits	API	Examples
Callable	object	()	All functions, methods, and lambdas
Container	object	in	bytearray, bytes, dict, frozenset, list, set, str, tuple
Hashable	object	hash()	bytes, frozenset, str, tuple
Iterable	object	iter()	bytearray, bytes, collections.deque, dict, frozenset, list, set, str, tuple
Iterator	Iterable	iter(), next()	
Sized	object	len()	bytearray, bytes, collections.deque, dict, frozenset, list, set, str, tuple
Mapping	Container, Iterable,	==, !=, [], len(), iter(), in, get(), items(), keys(),	dict

	Sized	values()	
Mutable-Mapping	Mapping	==, !=, [], del, len(), iter(), in, clear(), get(), items(), keys(), pop(), popitem(), setdefault(), update(), values()	dict
Sequence	Container, Iterable, Sized	[], len(), iter(), reversed(), in, count(), index()	bytearray, bytes, list, str, tuple
Mutable-Sequence	Container, Iterable, Sized	[], +=, del, len(), iter(), reversed(), in, append(), count(), extend(), index(), insert(), pop(), remove(), reverse()	bytearray, list
Set	Container, Iterable, Sized	<,<=, ==, !=, =>,>,&, |, ^, len(), iter(), in, isdisjoint()	frozenset, set
MutableSet	Set	<,<=, ==, !=, =>,>,&, |, ^, &=, |=, ^=, -=, len(), iter(), in, add(), clear(), discard(), isdisjoint(), pop(), remove()	set

The a b c statement that's needed by the abstractmethod() and abstractproperty() functions, as both can be used as decorators:

```
class Appliance(metaclass=abc.ABCMeta):

    @abc.abstractmethod

    def __init__(self, model, price):

        self.__model = model

        self.price = price


    def get_price(self):

        return self.__price


    def set_price(self, price):

        self.__price = price


    price = abc.abstractproperty(get_price, set_price)


    @property

    def model(self):

        return self.__model
```

We have set the class' metaclass to be abc. ABCMeta since this is a prerequisite for ABCs; any abc.ABCMeta subclass can be utilized rather, obviously. We have made __init__() an abstract technique to guarantee that it is reimplemented, and we have likewise given a usage which we expect (however can't compel) inheritors to call. To make an abstract coherent/writable property we can't utilize decorator syntax; additionally we have not utilized private names for the getter and setter since doing so would be awkward for subclasses.

The value property is abstract (so we can't utilize the @property decorator), and is meaningful/writable. Here we pursue a typical example for when we have private coherent/writable information (e.g., __price) as a property: We instate the property in the __init__() strategy as opposed to setting the private information straightforwardly—this guarantees the setter is called (and may possibly do approval or other work, even if it doesn't in this specific model).

The model property isn't abstract, so subclasses don't have to reimplement it, and we can make it a property utilizing the @property decorator. Here we pursue a typical example for when we have private perused just information (e.g., __model) as a property: now we set the private __model information once in the __init__() strategy, and give read get to by means of the read–just model property.

Note that no Appliance items can be made, on the grounds that the class contains abstract characteristics. Here is a model subclass:

class Cooker(Appliance):

def __init__(self, model, price, fuel): super().__init__(model, price)
self.fuel = fuel

price = property(lambda self: super().price,

lambda self, price: super().set_price(price))

The class called Cooker has to reimplement the __init__() strategy and the value property. For the property we have quite recently passed on all the work to the base class. The model read-just property is acquired. We could make a lot more classes dependent on Appliance, for example, Fridge, Toaster, etc.

The folliwing ABC we will look at is even shorter; it is an ABC for text-filtering functors (in file TextFilter.py):

```
class TextFilter(metaclass=abc.ABCMeta):

@abc.abstractproperty

def is_transformer(self):

raise NotImplementedError()

@abc.abstractmethod

def __call__(self):

raise NotImplementedError()
```

The TextFilter ABC gives no usefulness by any stretch of the imagination; it exists simply to characterize an interface, for this situation an is_transformer read-just property and a __call__() technique, that every one of its subclasses must give. Since the unique property and strategy have no usage we don't need subclasses to call them, so as opposed to utilizing a harmless pass proclamation we raise a special case in the event that they are utilized (e.g., by means of a super() call).

Here is one simple subclass:

```
class CharCounter(TextFilter):

@property

def is_transformer(self):

return False


def __call__(self, text, chars):

count = 0

for c in text:
```

```
if c in chars:

    count += 1

return count
```

This content channel isn't a transformer in light of the fact that instead of changing the content it is given, it basically restores a check of the predetermined characters that happen in the content.
Here is a case use case:

```
vowel_counter = CharCounter()

vowel_counter("dog fish and cat fish", "aeiou") # returns: 5
```

Two more filters are provided, both of which are transformers: RunLength-

Encode and RunLengthDecode. Here is how they are used:

```
rle_encoder = RunLengthEncode()

rle_text = rle_encoder(text)

...

rle_decoder = RunLengthDecode()

original_text = rle_decoder(rle_text)
```

The run length encoder changes over a string into UTF-8 encoded bytes, and replaces 0x00 bytes with the arrangement 0x00, 0x01, 0x00, and any succession of three to 255 rehashed bytes with the grouping 0x00, tally, byte. In the event that the string has loads of keeps running of at least four indistinguishable sequential characters this can deliver a shorter byte string than the crude bytes.
The decoder gets a run length encoded byte string and returns the first string. Here is the beginning of the RunLengthDecode class:

```python
class RunLengthDecode(TextFilter):

    @property
    def is_transformer(self):
        return True

    def __call__(self, rle_bytes):
        ...
```

We have discarded the body of the __call__() strategy, in spite of the fact that it is in the source that goes with this book. The RunLengthEncode class has the very same structure.

The last ABC we will take a gander at gives an Application Programming Interface (API) and a default usage for a fix component. Here is the finished ABC (from document Abstract.py):

```python
class Undo(metaclass=abc.ABCMeta):

    @abc.abstractmethod
    def __init__(self):
        self.__undos = []

    @abc.abstractproperty
    def can_undo(self):
        return bool(self.__undos)

    @abc.abstractmethod
    def undo(self):
        assert self.__undos, "nothing left to undo"
```

189

```
self.__undos.pop()(self)

def add_undo(self, undo):

self.__undos.append(undo)
```

The __init__() and fix() strategies must be reimplemented since they are both unique; thus should the read-just can_undo property. Subclasses don't need to reimplement the add_undo() technique, despite the fact that they are allowed to do as such. The fix() strategy is marginally unpretentious. The self.__undos rundown is relied upon to hold article references to strategies. Every technique must reason the comparing activity to be fixed on the off chance that it is called—this will be more clear when we take a gander at an Undo subclass in a minute. So to play out a fix we pop the last fix strategy off the self.__undos rundown, and after that call the technique as a capacity, passing self as a contention. (We should pass self on the grounds that the strategy is being called as a capacity and not as a technique.)

Here is the start of the Stack class; it acquires Undo, so any activities per-shaped on it tends to be fixed by calling Stack.undo() without any contentions:

```
class Stack(Undo):

def __init__(self):

super().__init__()

self.__stack = []

@property

def can_undo(self):

return super().can_undo

def undo(self):

super().undo()
```

```
def push(self, item):

self.__stack.append(item)

self.add_undo(lambda self: self.__stack.pop())

def pop(self):

item = self.__stack.pop()

self.add_undo(lambda self: self.__stack.append(item))

return item
```

We have excluded Stack.top() and Stack.__str__() since neither includes anything new and neither interfaces with the Undo base class. For the can_undo property and the fix() strategy, we just pass on the work to the base class. In the event that these two were not extract we would not have to reimplement them at all and a similar impact would be accomplished; however for this situation we needed to drive subclasses to reimplement them to urge fix to be assessed in the subclass. For push() and pop() we play out the activity and furthermore add a capacity to the fix list which will fix the activity that has quite recently been performed.

Dynamic base classes are most valuable in enormous scale projects, libraries, and application structures, where they can help guarantee that regardless of execution subtleties or creator, classes can work agreeably together in light of the fact that they give the APIs that their ABCs indicate.

Multiple Inheritance

Different legacy is the place one class acquires from at least two different classes. In spite of the fact that Python (and, for instance, C++) completely underpins different legacy, a few dialects—most outstandingly, Java—don't permit it. One issue is that various legacy can prompt a similar class being acquired more than once, and this implies the rendition of a technique that is called, on the off chance that it isn't in the subclass however is in at least two of the base classes (or their base classes, and so on.), relies upon the strategy goals request, which conceivably makes classes that utilization different legacy to some degree delicate.

Numerous legacy can for the most part be maintained a strategic distance from by utilizing single legacy (one base class), and setting a metaclass in the event that we need to help an extra API, since as we will find in the following subsection, a metaclass can be utilized to give the guarantee of an API without really acquiring any techniques or information properties. An option is to utilize different legacy with one solid class and at least one conceptual base classes for extra APIs. Furthermore, another option is to utilize single legacy and total cases of different classes.

In any case, sometimes, different legacy can give an advantageous arrangement. For instance, assume we need to make another adaptation of the Stack class from the past subsection, however need the class to help stacking and sparing utilizing a pickle. We may well need to include the stacking and sparing usefulness to a few classes, so we will actualize it in its very own class:

class LoadSave:

def __init__(self, filename, *attribute_names): self.filename = filename self.__attribute_names = []

for name in attribute_names:

if name.startswith("__"):

name = "_" + self.__class__.__name__ + name
self.__attribute_names.append(name)

def save(self):

with open(self.filename, "wb") as fh:

data = []

for name in self.__attribute_names:

```
data.append(getattr(self, name))

pickle.dump(data, fh, pickle.HIGHEST_PROTOCOL)

def load(self):

with open(self.filename, "rb") as fh:

data = pickle.load(fh)

for name, value in zip(self.__attribute_names, data):

setattr(self, name, value)
```

This class has two qualities: filename, which is open and can be changed whenever, and __attribute_names, which is fixed and can be set just when the example is made. The spare() strategy repeats over all the trait names and makes a rundown considered information that holds the estimation of each credit to be spared; it at that point spares the information into a pickle. The with articulation guarantees that the document is shut on the off chance that it was effectively opened, and any record or pickle special cases are left behind to the guest. The heap() technique repeats over the quality names and the comparing information things that have been stacked and sets each credit to its stacked worth.

Here is the beginning of the FileStack class that increase acquires the Undo class from the past subsection and this present subsection's LoadSave class:

```
class FileStack(Undo, LoadSave):

def __init__(self, filename):

Undo.__init__(self)

LoadSave.__init__(self, filename, "__stack")

self.__stack = []

def load(self):
```

193

```
super().load()
```

```
self.clear()
```

The remainder of the class is only equivalent to the Stack class, so we have not repro-duced it here. Rather than utilizing super() in the __init__() technique we should spec-ify the base classes that we introduce since super() can't figure our goals. For the LoadSave introduction we pass the filename to utilize and furthermore the names of the characteristics we need spared; for this situation only one, the private __stack. (We would prefer not to spare the __undos; and nor might we be able to for this situation since it is a rundown of strategies and is consequently unpicklable.)

 The FileStack class has all the Undo strategies, and furthermore the LoadSave class' spare() and burden() techniques. We have not reimplemented spare() since it works fine, yet for burden() we should clear the fix stack in the wake of stacking. This is fundamental since we may do a spare, at that point do different changes, and afterward a heap. The heap clears out what went previously, so any undos never again bode well. The first Undo class didn't have an unmistakable() technique, so we needed to include one:

```
def clear(self):
```

```
self.__undos = []
```

```
# In class Undo
```

 In the Stack.load() strategy we have utilized super() to call LoadSave.load() be-cause there is no Undo.load() technique to cause vagueness. In the event that both base class-es had a heap() strategy, the one that would get called would rely upon Python's technique goals request. We want to utilize super() just when there is no uncertainty, and to utilize the suitable base name generally, so we never depend on the technique goals request. For the self.clear() call, again there is no vagueness since just the Undo class has a reasonable() strategy, and we don't have to utilize super() since (in contrast to stack()) FileStack doesn't have an unmistakable() technique.

What might occur if, later on, a reasonable() strategy was added to the FileStack class? It would break the heap() strategy. One arrangement is call su-per().clear() inside burden() rather than plain self.clear(). This would result inthe first super-class' reasonable() strategy that was found being utilized. To ensure against such issues we could make it a strategy to utilize hard-coded base classes when utilizing numerous legacy (in this model, calling Undo.clear(self)). Or on the other hand we could stay away from different legacy inside and out and use collection, for test ple, acquiring the Undo class and making a LoadSave class intended for aggre-gation.

What different legacy has given us here is a blend of two rather dif-ferent classes, without the need to execute any of the fix or the stacking and sparing ourselves, depending rather on the usefulness given by the base classes. This can be helpful and works particularly well when the inher-ited classes have no covering APIs.

The metaclass

A metaclass is, for a class, what a class is to an example; that is, a metaclass is utilized to make classes, similarly as classes are utilized to make occasions. What's more, similarly as we can ask whether an example has a place with a class by utilizing isinstance(), we can ask whether a class object, (for example, dict, int, or SortedList) acquires another class utilizing issubclass().

The simplest use of metaclasses is to create custom classes that fit into Python's standard ABC hierarchy. For example, to make SortedList a collections.

So... instead of inheriting the ABC (as we showed earlier), we can simplyregister the SortedList as a collections.Sequence:

class SortedList:

...

collections.Sequence.register(SortedList)

After the class is characterized typically, we register it with the collections.Sequence ABC. Enlisting a class like this makes it a virtual subclass. A virtual sub-class reports that it is a subclass of the class or classes it is enlisted with (e.g., utilizing isinstance() or issubclass()), however doesn't acquire any information or techniques from any of the classes it is enrolled with.

Enlisting a class like this gives a guarantee that the class gives the API of the classes it is enrolled with, yet doesn't give any ensure that it will respect its guarantee. One utilization of metaclasses is to give both a guarantee and an assurance about a class' API. Another utilization is to change a class somehow or another (like a class decorator does). Furthermore, obviously, metaclasses can be utilized for the two purposes simultaneously.

Assume we need to make a gathering of classes that all give burden() and spare() techniques. We can do that by creating a class that when utilized as a metaclass, watches that these strategies are available:

class LoadableSaveable(type):

def __init__(cls, classname, bases, dictionary):
super().__init__(classname, bases, dictionary) assert hasattr(cls, "load") and \

isinstance(getattr(cls, "load"), collections.Callable), ("class '" + classname + "' must provide a load() method")

assert hasattr(cls, "save") and \

isinstance(getattr(cls, "save"), collections.Callable), ("class '" + classname + "' must provide a save() method")

Classes that are to fill in as metaclasses must acquire from a definitive metaclass base class, type, or one of its subclasses.

Notice that this class is called when classes that utilization it are started up, without a doubt not all the time, so the runtime cost is incredibly low. Notice additionally that we should play out the checks after the class has been made (utilizing the super() call), since at exactly that point will the class' properties be accessible in the classitself. (The qualities are in the word reference, yet we like to chip away at the genuine instated class when doing checks.)

We could have watched that the heap and spare properties are callable utilizing hasattr() to watch that they have the __call__ quality, yet we favor tocheck whether they are cases of collections.Callable. The collections.Callable unique base class gives the guarantee (however no assurance) thatinstances of its subclasses (or virtual subclasses) are callable.

When the class has been made (utilizing type.__new__() or a reimplementation of __new__()), the metaclass is introduced by calling its __init__() technique. The contentions given to __init__() are cls, the class that is simply been made; classname, the class' name (likewise accessible from cls.__name__); bases, a rundown ofthe class' base classes (barring object, and along these lines potentially vacant); and word reference that holds the traits that progressed toward becoming class properties when the cls class was made, except if we mediated in a reimplementation of the meta-class' __new__() strategy.

Here are two or three intuitive models that show what happens when we make classes utilizing the LoadableSaveable metaclass:

>>> class Bad(metaclass=Meta.LoadableSaveable):

... def some_method(self): pass Traceback (most recent call last):
...

AssertionError: class 'Bad' must provide a load() method
197

The metaclass specifies that classes using it should provide certain methods, and when they don't an AssertionError exception is raised.

```
>>> class Good(metaclass=Meta.LoadableSaveable):

...def load(self): pass

...def save(self): pass

>>> g = Good()
```

The Good class respects the metaclass' API prerequisites, regardless of whether it doesn't live up to our casual desires of how it ought to act.

We can likewise utilize metaclasses to change the classes that utilization them. In the event that the change includes the name, base classes, or word reference of the class being made (e.g., its spaces), at that point we have to reimplement the metaclass' __new__() strategy; yet for different changes, for example, including techniques or information qualities, reimplementing __init__() is adequate, despite the fact that this should likewise be possible in __new__(). We will nowlook at a metaclass that alters the classes it is utilized with absolutely through its __new__() strategy.

As an alternative to using this @property and @*name*.setter, we may code classes where we use a naming convention to distinguish properties. As an example, if a class owns methods of the form get_*name()* and set_*name()*, we can expect the class to have a private __*name* property accessed using *instance.name* for getting and setting. This can even be done with a metaclass.

Here is a sample of a class using this technique:

```
class Product(metaclass=AutoSlotProperties):

def __init__(self, barcode, description): self.__barcode = barcode
self.description = description

def get_barcode(self):
```

```python
return self.__barcode

def get_description(self):

return self.__description

def set_description(self, description):

if description is None or len(description) < 3:

self.__description = "<Invalid Description>"

else:

self.__description = description
```

We should dole out to the private __barcode property in the initializer since there is no setter for it; another result of this is standardized identification is a perused just property. Then again, portrayal is a decipherable/writable property. Here are a few instances of intelligent use:

```
>>> product = Product("101110110", "8mm Stapler")

>>> product.barcode, product.description ('101110110', '8mm Stapler')
>>> product.description = "8mm Stapler (long)"

>>> product.barcode, product.description ('101110110', '8mm Stapler (long)')
```

On the off chance that we endeavor to dole out to the standardized identification an AttributeError exemption is raised with the mistake content "can't set property".

On the off chance that we take a gander at the Product class' characteristics (e.g., utilizing dir()), the main open ones to be found are standardized identification and depiction. The get_name() and set_name() strategies are no longer there—they have been supplanted with the name property. What's more, the factors holding the scanner tag and portrayal are likewise private (__bar-code and __description), and have been added as openings to limit the class'smemory use. This is altogether done by the

AutoSlotProperties metaclass which is im-plemented in a solitary technique:

```
class AutoSlotProperties(type):

    def __new__(mcl, classname, bases, dictionary):

        slots = list(dictionary.get("__slots__", []))


        for getter_name in [key for key in dictionary if key.startswith("get_")]:
            if isinstance(dictionary[getter_name], collections.Callable):
                name = getter_name[4:]

        slots.append("__" + name)

        getter = dictionary.pop(getter_name)

        setter_name = "set_" + name

        setter = dictionary.get(setter_name, None)

        if (setter is not None and

        isinstance(setter, collections.Callable)):

        del dictionary[setter_name]

        dictionary[name] = property(getter, setter)

        dictionary["__slots__"] = tuple(slots)

        return super().__new__(mcl, classname, bases, dictionary)
```

A metaclass' __new__() class technique is called with the metaclass, and the class name, base classes, and word reference of the class that will be made. We should utilize a reimplementation of __new__() instead of __init__() in light of the fact that we need to change the word reference before the class is made.

We start by duplicating the __slots__ accumulation, making a vacant one if none is available, and ensuring we have a rundown instead of a tuple with the goal that we can change it. For each quality in the word reference we choose those that start with "get_" and that can be called, that is, those that are getter strategies. For every getter we have, we add a private name to the spaces to store the comparing information; for instance, given getter get_name() we add __name to the openings. We at that point take a reference to the getter and erase it from the lexicon under its unique name (this is done in one go utilizing dict.pop()). We do likewise for the setter on the off chance that one is available, and afterward we make another word reference thing with the ideal property name as its key; for instance, if the getter is get_name() the property name will be name. We set the thing's an incentive to be a property with the getter and setter (whichmight be None) that we have found and expelled from the word reference.

Toward the end we supplant the first spaces with the adjusted openings list which has a private space for every property that was included, and approach the base class to air conditioning tually make the class, however utilizing our changed word reference. Note that for this situation we should pass the metaclass unequivocally in the super() call; this is consistently the situation for calls to __new__() in light of the fact that it is a class strategy and not an occasion technique.

For this model we didn't have to compose a __init__() technique since we have done practically everything in __new__(), yet it is consummately conceivable to reimplement both __new__() and __init__() doing diverse work in each.

On the off chance that we consider hand-wrenched drills to be practically equivalent to accumulation and inher-itance and electric penetrates the simple of decorators and descriptors, at that point meta-classes are at the laser pillar end of the scale with regards to control and

adaptability. Metaclasses are the last apparatus to go after as opposed to the main, ex-cept maybe for application structure engineers who need to give control ful offices to their clients without causing the clients to experience bands to understand the advantages on offer.

Chapter 4: Functional-Style Programming

On the off chance that we consider hand-wrenched drills to be practically equivalent to accumulation and inher-itance and electric penetrates the simple of decorators and descriptors, at that point meta-classes are at the laser pillar end of the scale with regards to control and

adaptability. Metaclasses are the last apparatus to go after as opposed to the main, except maybe for application structure engineers who need to give control ful offices to their clients without causing the clients to experience bands to understand the advantages on offer.

```
list(map(lambda x: x ** 2, [1, 2, 3, 4]))          # returns: [1, 4, 9, 16]
```

The guide() work takes a capacity and an iterable as its contentions and for proficiency it restores an iterator as opposed to a rundown. Here we constrained a rundown to be made to make the outcome more clear:

```
[x ** 2 for x in [1, 2, 3, 4]]          # returns: [1, 4, 9, 16]
```

A generator articulation can regularly be utilized instead of guide(). Here we have utilized a rundown perception to stay away from the need to utilize list(); to make it a generator we simply need to change the external sections to enclosures.

Sifting includes taking a capacity and an iterable and delivering another iterable where every thing is from the first iterable - giving the capacity profits True when required the thing. The inherent channel() work sup-ports this:

```
list(filter(lambda x: x > 0, [1, -2, 3, -4])) # returns: [1, 3]
```

This filter() function gets a function and an iterable item as arguments and returns an iterator.

[x for x in [1, -2, 3, -4] if x > 0]   # returns: [1, 3]

The channel() capacity can generally be supplanted with a generator articulation or with a rundown appreciation.

Decreasing includes taking a capacity and an iterable and delivering a solitary outcome esteem. The manner in which this works is that the capacity is approached the iterable's initial two qualities, at that point on the processed outcome and the third worth, at that point on the figured outcome and the fourth worth, etc, until every one of the qualities have been utilized. The functools module's functools.reduce() work bolsters this. There are two lines of code that do a similar calculation:

functools.reduce(lambda x, y: x * y, [1, 2, 3, 4])   # returns: 24

functools.reduce(operator.mul, [1, 2, 3, 4])   # returns: 24

This operator module has a function for all of Python's operators specifically to make functional programming easier.

Now, in the second line, we used the operator.mul() function instead of creating a multiplication function using a lambda as we did earlier.

Python provides built-in reducing functions: all(), which, if given an iterable, returns True if all the iterable's items return True when bool() is applied to them; any(), which returns True if any of the iterable's items is True; max(), which returns the largest item in the iterable; min(), which returns thesmallest item in the iterable; and sum(), which returns the sum of the iterables.

Now we have covered the key concepts, let's look at a few examples.

We'll start with a couple of ways to get the total size of all the files in a list file:

```
functools.reduce(operator.add, (os.path.getsize(x) for x in files))
```

```
functools.reduce(operator.add, map(os.path.getsize, files))
```

We're using map() because it's shorter than the equivalent list comprehension, except when there's a condition.

Then, we used operator.add() as addition instead of lambda x, y: x + y.

If we wanted to count the .py file sizes we can filter out non-Python files.

Here are 3 different ways to do this:

```
functools.reduce(operator.add, map(os.path.getsize, filter(lambda x: x.endswith(".py"), files)))
```

```
functools.reduce(operator.add, map(os.path.getsize,
```

```
(x for x in files if x.endswith(".py")))))
```

```
functools.reduce(operator.add, (os.path.getsize(x)
```

```
for x in files if x.endswith(".py")))
```

Ostensibly, the second and third forms are better since they don't expect us to make a lambda work, however the decision between utilizing generator articulations (or rundown understandings) and guide() and channel() is frequently absolutely a matter of individual programming style.

Utilizing map(), channel(), and functools.reduce() regularly prompts the disposal of circles, as the models we have seen show. These capacities are valuable when changing over code written in a useful language, however in Python we can more often than not supplant map() with a rundown perception and channel() with a rundown cognizance with a condition, and numerous instances of functools.reduce() can be killed by utilizing one of Python's worked in practical capacities, for example, all(), any(), maximum(), min(), and whole(). For instance:

```
sum(os.path.getsize(x) for x in files if x.endswith(".py"))
```

That accomplishes a similar thing as the past three models, however is substantially more minimal.

Notwithstanding giving capacities to Python's administrators, the administrator module additionally gives the operator.attrgetter() and operator.itemgetter() capacities, the first we quickly met before in this section. Both of these arrival capacities which would then be able to be called to extricate the predefined traits or things.

While cutting can be utilized to separate an arrangement of part of a rundown, and cutting with striding can be utilized to remove a succession of parts (state, each third thing with L[::3]), operator.itemgetter() can be utilized to extricate a grouping of arbitrary parts, for instance, operator.itemgetter(4, 5, 6, 11, 18)(L) . The capacity returned by operator.itemgetter() doesn't need to be summoned promptly and tossed as we have done here; it could be kept and go as the capacity contention to delineate(), or functools.reduce(), or utilized in a word reference, rundown, or set cognizance.

When we need to sort we can indicate a key capacity. This capacity can be any capacity, for instance, a lambda work, an implicit capacity or strategy, (for example, str.lower()), or a capacity returned by operator.attrgetter(). For instance, expecting list L holds objects with a need quality, we can sort the rundown into need request this way: L.sort(key=operator.attrgetter("priority")).

Notwithstanding the functools and administrator modules previously referenced, the iter-apparatuses module can likewise be valuable for practical style programming. For test ple, despite the fact that it is conceivable to emphasize more than at least two records by linking them, an option is to utilize itertools.chain() like that:

for value in itertools.chain(data_list1, data_list2, data_list3):

total += value

The itertools.chain() function can return an iterator giving successive values from the first sequence, then successive values from the second one, and so on.

Partial Function Application

Halfway capacity application is the making of a capacity from a current capacity and a few contentions to create another capacity that does what the first capacity did, yet with certain contentions fixed so guests don't need to pass them. Here's a basic model:

enumerate1 = functools.partial(enumerate, start=1)

for lino, line in enumerate1(lines):

process_line(i, line)

The first line makes another capacity, enumerate1(), that wraps the given func-tion (identify()) and a catchphrase contention (start=1) so when enumerate1() is called it calls the first capacity with the fixed contention—and with whatever other contentions that are given at the time it is called, for this situation lines. Here we have utilized the enumerate1() capacity to give regular line tallying beginning from line 1.

Utilizing fractional capacity application can improve our code, particularly when we need to call similar capacities with similar contentions over and over. For instance, rather than determining the mode and encoding contentions each time we call open() to process UTF-8 encoded content records, we could make several capacities with these contentions fixed:

```
reader = functools.partial(open, mode="rt", encoding="utf8")
```

```
writer = functools.partial(open, mode="wt", encoding="utf8")
```

Now we can open text files for reading by calling reader(*filename*) and for writing by calling writer(*filename*).

One basic use case for halfway capacity application is in GUI (Graphical User Interface) programming where it is regularly conve-nient to have one specific capacity considered when any of a lot of catches is squeezed. For instance:

```
loadButton = tkinter.Button(frame, text="Load",
command=functools.partial(doAction, "load"))
```

```
saveButton = tkinter.Button(frame, text="Save",
command=functools.partial(doAction, "save"))
```

The example applies the tkinter GUI library that is a standard one on Python.

The tkinter.Button class is used to draw buttons—here we have created two, both are kept inside the same frame, and each of them has a text that indicates their purpose.

Every button's function argument is set to the name of the function that tkinter must call when the button is activated, in this case the doAction()

function. We used partial function application to make sure that the first argument for the doAction() function will be a string that indicates which button called it.

Cor
outi
nes

ic articulation, at that point suspend execution while hanging tight for certain information. Now different pieces of the program can keep on executing (normally different coroutines that aren't suspended). When the information is gotten the coroutine resumes from the point it was suspended, performs preparing (probably dependent on the information it got), and perhaps sending its outcomes to another coroutine. Coroutines are said to have different section and leave focuses, since they can have more than one spot where they suspend and continue.

Coro
utines
are
functi
ons
whos
e
prepa
ring
can
be
suspe
nded
and
conti
nued
at
expli
cit
focus
es. In
this
way,
ordin
arily,
a
corou
tine
will
execu
te up
to a
specif

Coroutines are helpful when we need to apply various functions to similar bits of information, or when we need to make information handling pipelines, or when we need to have an ace capacity with slave capacities. Coroutines can likewise be utilized to give less complex and lower-overhead options in contrast to stringing. A couple coroutine-based bundles that give lightweight stringing are accessible from the Python Package Index, pypi.python.org/pypi.

In Python, a coroutine is a function that takes its contribution from a yield articulation. It might likewise send results to a recipient work (which itself must be a corou-tine). At whatever point a coroutine arrives at a yield articulation it suspends sitting tight for information; and once it gets information, it resumes execution starting there. A corou-tine can have more than one yield articulation, albeit each of the coroutine models we will audit has just one.

Performing Independent Actions on Data

On the off chance that we need to play out a lot of autonomous activities on certain information, the ordinary methodology is to apply every activity thus. The weakness of this is in the event that one of the tasks is moderate, the program in general should trust that the activity will finish before going on to the following one. An answer for this is to utilize coroutines. We can execute every activity as a coroutine and afterward start them all off. In the event that one is moderate it won't influence the others—in any event not until they come up short on information to process—since they all work autonomously.

The figure below illustrates the use of coroutines for concurrent processing. In the fig-ure, three coroutines (each presumably doing a different job) process the same two data items—and take different amounts of time to do their work. In the figure, coroutine1()

212

works quite quickly, coroutine2() works slowly, and corou- tine3() varies. Once all three coroutines have been given their initial data

Step	Action	coroutine1()	coroutine2()	coroutine3()
1	Create coroutines	Waiting	Waiting	Waiting
2	coroutine1.send("a")	Process "a"	Waiting	Waiting
3	coroutine2.send("a")	Process "a"	Process "a"	Waiting
4	coroutine3.send("a")	Waiting	Process "a"	Process "a"
5	coroutine1.send("b")	Process "b"	Process "a"	Process "a"
6	coroutine2.send("b")	Process "b"	Process "a" ("b" pending)	Process "a"
7	coroutine3.send("b")	Waiting	Process "a" ("b" pending)	Process "b"
8		Waiting	Process "b"	Process "b"
9		Waiting	Process "b"	Waiting
10		Waiting	Process "b"	Waiting
11		Waiting	Waiting	Waiting
12	coroutine*N*.close()	Finished	Finished	Finished

214

to process, if one is ever waiting (because it finishes first), the others continue to work, which minimizes processor idle time. Once we are finished using the coroutines we call close() on each of them; this stops them from waiting for more data, which means they won't consume any more processor time.

To make a coroutine in Python, we essentially make a function that has in any event one yield articulation—typically inside an unbounded circle. At the point when a yield is arrived at the coroutine's execution is suspended sitting tight for information. When the information is gotten the coroutine resumes preparing (from the yield articulation onward), and when it has completed it circles back to the respect hang tight for more information. While at least one coroutines are suspended sitting tight for information, another can execute. This can create more noteworthy throughput than basically executing functions in a steady progression directly.

We will demonstrate how performing autonomous activities functions by and by applying a few ordinary articulations to the content in a lot of HTML documents. The design is to yield each document's URLs and level 1 and level 2 headings. We'll begin by taking a gander at the standard articulations, at that point the production of the coroutine "matchers", and afterward we will take a gander at the coroutines and how they are utilized.

```
URL_RE = re.compile(r"""href=(?P<quote>["'])(?P<url>[^\1]+?)"""
                    r"""(?P=quote)""", re.IGNORECASE)

flags = re.MULTILINE|re.IGNORECASE|re.DOTALL


H1_RE = re.compile(r"<h1>(?P<h1>.+?)</h1>", flags)


H2_RE = re.compile(r"<h2>(?P<h2>.+?)</h2>", flags)
```

215

These standard articulations ("regexes" starting now and into the foreseeable future) coordinate a HTML href's URL and the content contained in <h1> and <h2> header labels. (Standard articulations are shrouded in Chapter 13; understanding them isn't fundamental to understanding this model.)

```
receiver = reporter()

matchers = (regex_matcher(receiver, URL_RE),
                regex_matcher(receiver, H1_RE),
                regex_matcher(receiver, H2_RE))
```

Since coroutines consistently have a yield articulation, they are generators. So albeit here we make a tuple of matcher coroutines, as a result we are making a tuple of generators. Each regex_matcher() is a coroutine that takes a beneficiary function (itself a coroutine) and a regex to coordinate. At whatever point the matcher matches it sends the match to the recipient.

```
@coroutine

def regex_matcher(receiver, regex):

    while True:

        text = (yield)

        for match in regex.finditer(text):

            receiver.send(match)
```

The matcher begins by entering a vast circle and promptly suspends execution trusting that the yield articulation will restore a book to apply the regex to. When the content is gotten, the matcher repeats over each match it makes, sending every one to the recipient.

When the coordinating has completed the coroutine circles back to the yield and again suspends hanging tight for more content.

There is one small issue with the (undecorated) matcher—when it is first made it ought to start execution so it advances to the yield prepared to get its first content. We could do this by calling the implicit next() function on each coroutine we make before sending it any information. Be that as it may, for accommodation we have made the @coroutine decorator to do this for us.

```python
def coroutine(function):


@functools.wraps(function)


def wrapper(*args, **kwargs):
```

```
generator = function(*args, **kwargs)


next(generator)


return generator


return wrapper
```

The @coroutine decorator gets a coroutine function, and calls the next() function on it—that causes the function to be processed up to the first expression.

Now that we seen the matcher coroutine we will look at how the matchers are used, and then we will look at the reporter() coroutine that receives the matchers' outputs.

```
try:


for file in sys.argv[1:]:


print(file)


html = open(file, encoding="utf8").read()


for matcher in matchers:
```

```
matcher.send(html)
```

```
finally:
```

```
for matcher in matchers:
```

```
matcher.close()
```

```
receiver.close()
```

The program peruses the filenames recorded on the direction line, and for every one prints the filename and afterward adds the document's whole content to the html variable utilizing the UTF-8 encoding. At that point the program repeats over every one of the matchers (three for this situation), and sends the content to every one of them. Every matcher at that point continues freely, sending each match it makes to the journalist coroutine. Toward the end we call close() on every matcher and on the correspondent—this ends them, since else they would proceed (suspended) hanging tight for content (or matches on account of the journalist) since they contain unbounded circles.

```
@coroutine
```

```
def reporter():
```

```
ignore = frozenset({"style.css", "favicon.png", "index.html"})
```

```
while True:
```

```python
match = (yield)

if match is not None:

    groups = match.groupdict()

    if "url" in groups and groups["url"] not in ignore:

        print("      URL:", groups["url"])

    elif "h1" in groups:

        print("      H1: ", groups["h1"])

    elif "h2" in groups:

        print("      H2: ", groups["h2"])
```

The columnist() coroutine is utilized to yield results. It was made by the state-ment beneficiary = correspondent() which we saw prior, and go as the recipient contention to every one of the matchers. The correspondent() pauses (is suspended) until a match is sent to it, at that point it prints the match's subtleties, and afterward it stands by once more, in an interminable circle—halting just assuming close() is approached it.

Utilizing coroutines like this may deliver execution benefits, yet requires us to embrace a to some degree diverse perspective about preparing.

221

Chapter 5: DEBUGGING, TESTING AND PROFILING

Composing projects is a blend of workmanship, specialty, and science, and on the grounds that it is finished by people, botches are made. Luckily, there are strategies we can use to help maintain a strategic distance from issues in any case, and procedures for distinguishing and fixing botches when they become evident.

Missteps fall into a few classes. The speediest to uncover themselves and the most effortless to fix are punctuation blunders, since these are for the most part because of grammatical mistakes. Additional difficult are coherent mistakes—with these, the program runs, yet some part of its conduct isn't what we proposed or anticipated. Numerous mistakes of this sort can be kept from occurring by utilizing TDD (Test Driven Development), where when we need to include another component, we start by composing a test for the element—which will fall flat since we haven't included the element yet—and after that actualize the element itself. Another misstep is to make a program that has unnecessarily horrible showing. This is quite often because of a poor decision of calculation or information structure or both. In any case, before endeavoring any enhancement we should begin by discovering precisely where the exhibition bottleneck lies—since it probably won't be the place we expect—and after that we ought to painstakingly de-cide what advancement we need to do, instead of working indiscriminately.

In this present part's first segment we will take a gander at Python's tracebacks to perceive how to spot and fix grammar mistakes and how to manage unhandled special cases. At that point we will perceive how to apply the logical strategy to investigating to make discovering mistakes as quick and easy as would be prudent. We will likewise see Python's investigating support. In the second area we will see Python's help for composing unit tests, and specifically the doctest module and the unittest module. We will perceive how to utilize these modules to help TDD. In the part's last area we will quickly see profiling, to recognize execution problem areas with the goal that we can appropriately focus on our improvement endeavors.

Chapter 6: Debugging

In this segment we will start by taking a gander at what Python does when there is a sentence structure mistake, at that point at the tracebacks that Python produces when unhandled ex-ceptions happen, and afterward we will perceive how to apply the logical technique to investigate ging. In any case, before all that we will quickly examine reinforcements and adaptation control.

When altering a program to fix a bug there is consistently the hazard that we end up with a program that has the first bug in addition to new bugs, that is, it is far more terrible than it was the point at which we began! What's more, on the off chance that we haven't got any reinforcements (or we have yet they are a few changes outdated), and we don't utilize adaptation control, it could be extremely difficult to try and return to where we simply had the first bug.

Making ordinary reinforcements is a fundamental piece of programming—regardless of how solid our machine and working framework are and how uncommon disappointments are—since disappointments still happen. In any case, reinforcements will in general be coarse-grained, with records hours or even days old.

Variant control frameworks enable us to gradually spare changes at whatever degree of granularity we need—each and every change, or each arrangement of related changes, or essentially every such a significant number of minutes of work. Rendition control frameworks enable us to apply changes (e.g., to try different things with bugfixes), and in the event that they don't work out, we can return the progressions to the last "great" adaptation of the code. So before beginning to troubleshoot, it is in every case best to register our code with the rendition control framework so we have a known position that we can return to on the off chance that we get into a wreck.

There are numerous great cross-stage open source variant control frameworks accessible—this book utilizes (bazaar-vcs.org), however other well known ones incorporate Mercurial (mercurial.selenic.com), (git-scm.com), and Subversion (subversion.tigris.org). By chance, both Bazaar and Mercurial are for the most part written in Python. None of these frameworks is difficult to use (in any event for the essentials), yet utilizing any of them will help keep away from a ton of pointless torment.

Dealing with Syntax Errors

On the off chance that we attempt to run a program that has a punctuation blunder, Python will stop execution and print the filename, line number, and culpable line, with a caret (^) under-neath showing precisely where the mistake was distinguished. Here's a model:

File "blocks.py", line 383

if BlockOutput.save_blocks_as_svg(blocks, svg)

                                                    ^

SyntaxError: invalid syntax

Can you see the error? We forgot the colon at the end of the row with the if statement condition.

There is an example that comes up quite often, but where the problem isn't so obvious to understand:

File "blocks.py", line 385

except ValueError as err:

^

SyntaxError: invalid syntax

There is no grammar blunder in the line showed, so both the line number and the caret's position aren't right. By and large, when we are looked with a mistake that we are persuaded isn't in the predetermined line, in pretty much every case the blunder will be in a previous line. Here's the code from the attempt to the aside from where Python is detailing the mistake to be—check whether you can recognize the blunder before perusing the clarification that pursues this code:

try:

blocks = parse(blocks)

svg = file.replace(".blk", ".svg")

if not BlockOutput.save_blocks_as_svg(blocks, svg):

print("Error: failed to save {0}".format(svg)

except ValueError as err:

Do you recognize the issue? It is surely barely noticeable since it is at stake before the one that Python reports as having the mistake. We have

shut the str.format() strategy's enclosures, however not the print()
function's parentheses,that is, we are feeling the loss of an end bracket
toward the stopping point, yet Python didn't understand this until it came
to the with the exception of watchword on the accompanying line.
Missing the keep going enclosure on a line is very normal, particularly
when utilizing print() with str.format(), however the mistake is typically
investigated the followingline. Likewise, if a rundown's end section, or a
set or word reference's end support is missing, Python will typically
report the issue as being on the following (non-clear) line. On the in
addition to side, punctuation mistakes like these are insignificant to fix.

Dealing with Runtime Errors

On the off chance that an unhandled special case happens at runtime,
Python will quit executing our program and print a traceback. Here is a
case of a traceback for an unhandled special case:

Traceback (most recent call last):

File "blocks.py", line 392, in <module> main()

File "blocks.py", line 381, in main

blocks = parse(blocks)

File "blocks.py", line 174, in recursive_descent_parse return data.stack[1]
IndexError: list index out of range

The tracebacks (likewise called backtraces) like this ought to be perused from their last line back toward their first line. The last line indicates the unhandled exemption that happened. Over this line, the filename, line number, and function name, trailed by the line that caused the special case, are appeared (spread more than two lines). On the off chance that the function where the special case was raised was called by another function, that function's filename, line number, function name, and calling line are appeared previously. Furthermore, if that function was called by another function the equivalent applies, as far as possible up to the start of the call stack. (Note that the filenames in tracebacks are given with their way, yet as a rule we have precluded ways from the models for lucidity.)

So in this model, an IndexError happened, implying that data.stack is some sort of arrangement, however has no thing at position 1. The blunder happened at line 174 in the blocks.py program's recursive_descent_parse() function, so that function was called at line 381 in the fundamental() function. (The explanation that the function's name is diverse at line 381, that is, parse() rather than repeat sive_descent_parse(), is that the parse variable is set to one of a few differentfunctions relying upon the order line contentions given to the program; in the regular case the names consistently coordinate.) The call to principle() was made at line 392, and this is the announcement at which program execution initiated.

Despite the fact that from the outset locate the traceback looks threatening, presently that we under-stand its structure it is anything but difficult to perceive how valuable it is. For this situation it reveals to us ex-actly where to search for the issue, despite the fact that obviously we should work out for ourselves what the arrangement is.

Here is another model traceback:

Traceback (most recent call last):

File "blocks.py", line 392, in <module>

main()

File "blocks.py", line 383, in main

if BlockOutput.save_blocks_as_svg(blocks, svg):

File "BlockOutput.py", line 141, in save_blocks_as_svg

widths, rows = compute_widths_and_rows(cells, SCALE_BY) File "BlockOutput.py", line 95, in compute_widths_and_rows
width = len(cell.text) // cell.columns ZeroDivisionError: integer division or modulo by zero

Now, the problem occurred in a module (BlockOutput.py) that is called by the blocks.py program. This traceback leads us to where the problem became *apparent*, but not to where it *occurred*.

The estimation of cell.columns is plainly 0 in the BlockOutput.py module's compute_widths_and_rows() function on line 95—all things considered, that is the thing that made the ZeroDivisionError special case be raised—yet we should take a gander at the former lines to discover where and why cell.columns was given this off base worth.

Sometimes the traceback uncovers an exemption that happened in Python's standard library or in an outsider library. Despite the fact that this could mean a bug in the library, in pretty much every case it is because of a bug in our very own code. Here is a case of such a traceback, utilizing Python 3.0:

Traceback (most recent call last):

File "blocks.py", line 392, in <module>

main()

File "blocks.py", line 379, in main

blocks = open(file, encoding="utf8").read()

File "/usr/lib/python3.0/lib/python3.0/io.py", line 278, in __new__ return open(*args, **kwargs)
File "/usr/lib/python3.0/lib/python3.0/io.py", line 222, in open closefd)

File "/usr/lib/python3.0/lib/python3.0/io.py", line 619, in __init__ _fileio._FileIO.__init__(self, name, mode, closefd)
IOError: [Errno 2] No such file or directory: 'hierarchy.blk'

The IOError special case toward the end lets us know plainly what the issue is. In any case, the special case was increased in the expectation library's io module. In such cases it is ideal to continue perusing upward until we locate the primary document recorded that is our program's record (or one of the modules we have made for it). So for this situation we find that the principal reference to our program is to record blocks.py, line 379, in the primary() function. It would seem that we have a call to open() yet have not put the callinside an attempt ... aside from square or utilized a with proclamation.

Python 3.1 is somewhat more astute than Python 3.0 and understands that we need to discover the error in our own code, not in the standard library, so it creates a substantially more minimal and supportive traceback. For instance:

Traceback (most recent call last):

File "blocks.py", line 392, in <module>

main()

File "blocks.py", line 379, in main

blocks = open(file, encoding="utf8").read()

IOError: [Errno 2] No such file or directory: 'hierarchy.blk'

This kills all the superfluous detail and makes it simple to perceive what the issue is (on the primary concern) and where it happened (the lines over it).

So it doesn't matter how long the traceback is, the last line always specifies the unhan-dled exception, and we just have to work back until we find our program's file or the one of our own modules. The problem will almost certainly be on the line Python specifies, or on an earlier line.

This specific model outlines that we ought to alter the blocks.py program to adapt smoothly when given the names of nonexistent records. This is an ease of use mistake, and it ought to likewise be named a consistent blunder, since terminating and printing a traceback can't be viewed as satisfactory program conduct.

Indeed, as an issue of good arrangement and affability to our clients, we ought to consistently get every single applicable exemption, recognizing the particular ones that we consider to be conceivable, for example, EnvironmentError. When all is said in done, we ought not utilize the catchalls of aside from: or with the exception of Exception:, in spite of the fact that utilizing the last at the top degree of our program to keep away from accidents may be fitting—however just on the off chance that we generally report any special cases it gets so they don't go quietly unnoticed.

Special cases that we get and can't recoup from ought to be accounted for as blunder messages, instead of presenting our clients to tracebacks which look unnerving to the unenlightened. For GUI programs the equivalent applies, then again, actually ordinarily we would utilize a message box to tell the client of an issue. Furthermore, for server programs that typically run unattended, we ought to compose the blunder message to the server's log.

Python's exemption pecking order was structured with the goal that getting Exception doesn't exactly cover every one of the special cases. Specifically, it doesn't get the KeyboardInter-rupt exemption, so for comfort applications if the client presses Ctrl+C, the programwill end. In the event that we get this exemption, there is a hazard that we could secure the client in a program that they can't end. This emerges on the grounds that a bug in our special case taking care of code may keep the program from terminating or the exemption spreading. (Obviously, even a "uninterruptible" program can have its procedure slaughtered, however not all clients know how.) So in the event that we do get the KeyboardInterrupt exemption we should be very mindful so as to do the base measure of sparing and tidy up that is important—and afterward terminate the program. What's more, for projects that don't have to spare or tidy up, it is best not to get KeyboardInterrupt by any stretch of the imagination, and simply let the program end.

One of Python 3's incredible ideals is that it makes an obvious differentiation between crude bytes and strings. Be that as it may, this can some of the time lead to sudden exemptions happening when we pass a bytes object where a str is normal or the other way around. For instance:

Traceback (most recent call last):

```
File "program.py", line 918, in <module>
print(datetime.datetime.strptime(date, format))
TypeError: strptime() argument 1 must be str, not bytes
```

When you hit an issue like this we can either play out the change—for this situation, by passing date.decode("utf8")— or cautiously work back to discover whereand why the variable is a bytes object as opposed to a str, and fix the issue at the source.

If we pass a string while bytes are expected the error message is somewhat less obvious, and differs between Python 3.0 and 3.1. For example, in Python 3.0:

```
Traceback (most recent call last):

File "program.py", line 2139, in <module> data.write(info)
TypeError: expected an object with a buffer interface
```

In Python 3.1 the error message's text has been slightly improved:

```
Traceback (most recent call last):

File "program.py", line 2139, in <module> data.write(info)
TypeError: 'str' does not have the buffer interface
```

In the two cases the issue is that we are passing a string when a bytes, byte-exhibit, or comparable article is normal. We can either play out the change—inthis case by passing info.encode("utf8")— or work back to discover the wellspring of the issue and fix it there.

Python 3.0 presented support for special case binding—this implies an ex-ception that is brought up in light of another exemption can contain the subtleties of the first exemption. At the point when a fastened special case goes uncaught the traceback incorporates the uncaught exemption, yet in addition the special case that caused it (giving it was affixed). The way to deal with investigating tied special cases is al-most equivalent to previously: We start toward the end and work in reverse until we discover the issue in our very own code. In any case, instead of doing this only for the last special case, we may then recurrent the procedure for each tied exemption above it, until we get to the issue's actual beginning.

We can exploit exemption binding in our own code—for instance, in the event that we need to utilize a custom special case class yet at the same time need the hidden issue to be noticeable.

```
class InvalidDataError(Exception): pass

def process(data):

try:

i = int(data)

...

except ValueError as err:

raise InvalidDataError("Invalid data received") from err
```

Now, the int() conversion fails and the ValueError is called and caught. We then call our exception, but with from err, which creates a chained exception. If the exception is raised but not caught, the traceback will look like that:

```
Traceback (most recent call last):

File "application.py", line 249, in process i = int(data)
ValueError: invalid literal for int() with base 10: '17.5 '
```

The above exception was the direct cause of the following exception:

```
Traceback (most recent call last):
```

File "application.py", line 288, in <module> print(process(line))
File "application.py", line 283, in process

raise InvalidDataError("Invalid data received") from err
__main__.InvalidDataError: Invalid data received

The base our custom special case and content clarify what the issue is, with the lines above them demonstrating where the exemption was raised (line 283), and where it was caused (line 288). In any case, we can likewise return further, into the anchored exemption which gives more insights regarding the particular mistake, and which demonstrates the line that set off the special case (249).

Scientific Debugging

In the event that our program runs however doesn't have the normal or wanted conduct then we have a bug—an intelligent mistake—that we should dispense with. The most ideal approach to dispense with such blunders is to keep them from happening in any case by utilizing TDD (Test Driven Development). Be that as it may, a few bugs will consistently get past, so even with TDD, troubleshooting is as yet a vital aptitude to learn.

In this subsection we will diagram a way to deal with investigating dependent on the logical strategy. The methodology is clarified in adequate detail that it may ap-pear to be an excess of work for handling a "basic" bug. In any case, by deliberately following the procedure we will abstain from sitting around with "irregular" investigating, and after for a moment we will disguise the procedure so we can do it unknowingly, and consequently rapidly.

To fix a bug we need be able to...

1. Reproduce it.

2. Locate it.

3. Fix it.

4. Test.

Reproducing the bug is some of the time simple—it generally happens on each run; and in some cases hard—it happens irregularly. In either case we should attempt to diminish the bug's conditions, that is, locate the littlest info and minimal measure of preparing that can even now deliver the bug.

When we can replicate the bug, we have the information—the info information and alternatives, and the off base outcomes—that are required with the goal that we can apply the logical technique to finding and fixing it.

Running the investigation should find the bug, and ought to likewise give us understanding into its answer. (We will come back to how to make and run an analysis in no time.) Once we have chosen how to kill the bug—and have registered our code with our form control framework so we can return the fix if vital—we can compose the fix.

When events will play out as planned spot we should test it. Normally, we should test to check whether the bug it is expected to fix has left. Yet, this isn't adequate; all things considered, our fix may have illuminated the bug we were worried about, yet the fix may likewise have presented another bug, one that influences some other part of the program. So notwithstanding testing the bugfix, we should likewise run the majority of the program's tests to expand our certainty that the bugfix didn't have any undesirable reactions.

A few bugs have a specific structure, so at whatever point we fix a bug it is constantly worth inquiring as to whether there are different places in the program or its modules that may have comparable bugs. In the event that there are, we can verify whether we as of now have tests that would uncover the bugs on the off chance that they were available, and in the event that not, we should include such tests, and on the off chance that

that uncovers bugs, at that point we should handle them as depicted before.

Since we have a decent review of the investigating procedure, we will concentrate in on exactly how we make and run analyses to test our speculations. We start with attempting to separate the bug. Contingent upon the idea of the program and of the bug, we may have the option to compose tests that activity the program, for instance, bolstering it information that is known to be handled accurately and step by step changing the information so we can discover precisely where preparing falls flat. When we have a thought of where the issue lies—either because of testing or dependent on thinking—we can test our theories.

What sort of theory may we brainstorm? All things considered, it could at first be as sim-ple as the doubt that a specific function or technique is returning wrong information when certain info information and alternatives are utilized. At that point, if this speculation demonstrates right, we can refine it to be progressively explicit—for instance, distinguishing a specific proclamation or suite in the function that we believe is doing an inappropriate calculation in specific cases.

To test our speculation we have to check the contentions that the function receives and the estimations of its neighborhood factors and the arrival esteem, preceding it returns. We would then be able to run the program with information that we know master duces mistakes and check the speculate function. On the off chance that the contentions coming into the function are not what we expect, at that point the issue is probably going to be further up the call stack, so we would now start the procedure once more, this time presuming the function that calls the one we have been taking a gander at. In any case, in the event that all the approaching contentions are constantly substantial, at that point we should take a gander at the nearby factors and the arrival esteem. In the event that these are constantly right, at that point we have to think of another theory, since the presume function is acting accurately. In any case, on the off chance that the arrival worth isn't right, at that point we realize that we should explore the function further.

Practically speaking, how would we direct an investigation, that is, how would we test the theory that a specific function is acting mischievously? One approach to begin is to "execute" the function rationally—this is workable for some little functions and for bigger ones with training, and has the extra advantage that it acclimates us with the function's conduct. Best case scenario, this can prompt an improved or increasingly explicit theory—for instance, that a specific explanation or suite is the site of the issue. However, to direct an investigation appropriately we should instrument the program so we can perceive what is happening when the presume function is called.

There are two different ways to instrument a program—rudely, by embeddings print() proclamations; or (generally) non-rudely, by utilizing a debugger. The two methodologies are utilized to accomplish a similar end and both are substantial, yet a few software engineers have a solid inclination for either. We'll quickly depict the two approaches, beginning with the utilization of print() proclamations.

When utilizing print() proclamations, we can begin by putting a print() articulation directly toward the start of the function and have it print the function's contentions. At that point, just before the (or each) arrival explanation (or toward the finish of the function if there is no arrival articulation), include print(locals(), "\n"). The implicit local people() function restores a lexicon whose keys are the names of the nearby factors and whose qualities are the factors' qualities. We can obviously just print the factors we are explicitly inspired by. Notice that we included an extra newline—we ought to likewise do this in the main print() articulation with the goal that a clear line shows up between each arrangement of factors to help clearness.

The option in contrast to including print() explanations is to utilize a debugger. Python has two standard debuggers. One is provided as a module (pdb), and can be utilized intuitively in the comfort—for instance, python3 - m pdb my_program.py. (On Windows, obviously, we would supplant python3 with something like C:\Python31\python.exe.) However, the most straightforward approach to utilize it is to include import pdb in the program itself, and include the announcement pdb.set_trace() as the primary state-ment of the function we need to inspect. At the point when the program is run, pdb stops it following the pdb.set_trace() call, and enables us to step through the program, set breakpoints, and look at factors.

Here is a model kept running of a program that has been instrumented by having the import pdb articulation added to its imports, and by having pdb.set_trace() included as the primary proclamation inside its calculate_median() function. (What we have composed is appeared in striking, in spite of the fact that where we composed Enter isn't shown.)

python3 statistics.py sum.dat

> statistics.py(73)calculate_median() -> numbers = sorted(numbers)
(Pdb) **s**

> statistics.py(74)calculate_median() -> middle = len(numbers) // 2
(Pdb)

> statistics.py(75)calculate_median() -> median = numbers[middle]
(Pdb)

> statistics.py(76)calculate_median() -> if len(numbers) % 2 == 0:
(Pdb)

> statistics.py(78)calculate_median() -> return median
(Pdb) **p middle, median, numbers**

(8, 5.0, [-17.0, -9.5, 0.0, 1.0, 3.0, 4.0, 4.0, 5.0, 5.0, 5.0, 5.5, 6.0, 7.0, 7.0, 8.0, 9.0, 17.0])
(Pdb) c

Directions are given to pdb by entering their name and squeezing Enter at the (Pdb) brief. On the off chance that we simply press Enter individually the last direction is repeated.So here we composed s (which means step, i.e., execute the announcement appeared), and afterward rehashed this (basically by squeezing Enter), to step through the announcements in the calculate_median() function. When we arrived at the arrival articulation we printed out the qualities that intrigued us utilizing the p (print) direction. Lastly we proceeded to the end utilizing the c (proceed) direction. This minor model should give a kind of pdb, obviously the module has much more functionality than we have appeared here.

It is a lot simpler to utilize pdb on an instrumented program as we have done here than on a uninstrumented one. Yet, since this expects us to include an import and a call to pdb.set_trace(), doubtlessly utilizing pdb is similarly as nosy as utilizing print() proclamations, in spite of the fact that it provides helpful offices, for example, breakpoints.

Unit Testing

Composing tests for our projects—whenever progressed admirably—can help lessen the occurrence of bugs and can expand our certainty that our projects act true to form. In any case, when all is said in done, testing can't ensure rightness, since for most nontrivial programs the scope of potential sources of info and the scope of potential calculations is huge to such an extent that solitary the littlest part of them would ever be practically tried. Regardless, via cautiously picking what we test we can improve the nature of the code.

A great variety of kinds of testing techniques can be done, such as usability testing, functional testing, and integration testing. But here we will concern ourselves purely with unit testing—testing individual functions, classes, and methods, to ensure that they behave according to our expectations.

A key purpose of TDD, is that when we need to include an element—for instance, another technique to a class—we initially compose a test for it. Furthermore, obviously this test will come up short since we haven't composed the technique. Presently we compose the technique, and once it breezes through the test we would then be able to rerun every one of the tests to ensure our expansion hasn't had any startling symptoms. When every one of the tests run (counting the one we included for the new element), we can check in our code, sensibly sure that it does what we expect—giving obviously that our test was satisfactory.

If you have to create a function which inserts a string at an index position, you will start using TDD like this:

def insert_at(string, position, insert):

"""Returns a copy of string with insert inserted at the position

>>> string = "ABCDE"

```
>>> result = []

>>> for i in range(-2, len(string) + 2):

... result.append(insert_at(string, i, "-"))

>>> result[:5]

['ABC-DE', 'ABCD-E', '-ABCDE', 'A-BCDE', 'AB-CDE']

>>> result[5:]

['ABC-DE', 'ABCD-E', 'ABCDE-', 'ABCDE-']

"""

return string
```

For functions or strategies that don't return anything (they really return None), we typically give them a suite comprising of pass, and for those whose arrival worth is utilized we either return a consistent (state, 0) or one of the contentions, unaltered—which is the thing that we have done here. (In progressively complex circumstances it might be increasingly valuable to return phony articles—outsider modules that give "mock" objects are accessible for such cases.)

At the point when the doctest is run it will fall flat, posting every one of the strings ('ABCD-EF', 'ABCDE-F', and so on.) that it expected, and the strings it really got (all of whichare 'ABCDEF'). When we are fulfilled that the doctest is adequate and right, we can compose the body of the function, which for this situation is basically returnstring[:position] + embed + string[position:]. (Furthermore, on the off chance that we composed return string[:position] + supplement, and afterward reordered string[:position] atthe end to spare ourselves some composing, the doctest will quickly uncover the mistake.)

Python's standard library gives two unit testing modules, doctest, which we have as of now quickly observed here and before (in Chapter 5; 202 ►, and Chap-ter 6; 247 ►), and unittest. What's more, there are outsider trying instruments for Python. Two of the most striking are nose (code.google.com/p/python-nose), which expects to be more far reaching and valuable than the standard unit-test module, while as yet being perfect with it, and py.test (codespeak. net/py/dist/test/test.html)— this adopts a to some degree diverse strategy to unittest, and attempts however much as could be expected to dispense with standard test code. Bothof these outsider apparatuses bolster test revelation, so there is no compelling reason to compose a general test program—since they will scan for tests themselves. This makes it simple to test a whole tree of code or only a piece of the tree (e.g., simply those modules that have been chipped away at). For those genuine about testing it merits researching both of these outsider modules (and any others that intrigue), before choosing which testing instruments to utilize.

It's pretty easy to create doctests: We write the tests in the module, function, class or methods' docstrings, or about modules, we just add these lines after the code:

if __name__ == "__main__":

import doctest

doctest.testmod()

If you need to use doctests inside the program, that's entirely possible. For instance, the blocks.py file has doctests for its functions, it ends with this code:

if __name__ == "__main__":

main()

This essentially calls the program's principle() function, and doesn't execute the program's doctests. To practice the program's doctests there are two ap-proaches we can follow. The first is importing the doctest module and afterward run the program—for instance, at the reassure, python3 - m doctest blocks.py (on Win-dows, supplanting python3 with something like C:\Python31\python.exe). On the off chance that every one of the tests run fine there is no yield, so we may like to execute python3 - mdoctest blocks.py - v rather, since this will list each doctest that is executed,and give a rundown of results toward the end.

Another approach to execute doctests is to make a different test program utilizing the unittest module. The unittest module is theoretically displayed on Java's JUnit unit testing library and is utilized to make test suites that contain experiments. The unittest module can make experiments dependent on doctests, without knowing anything about what the program or module contains, aside from the way that it has doctests. So to make a test suite for the blocks.py program, we can make the accompanying straightforward program (which we have called test_blocks.py):

import doctest

import unittest

import blocks

 suite = unittest.TestSuite()

suite.addTest(doctest.DocTestSuite(blocks))

runner = unittest.TextTestRunner()

print(runner.run(suite))

Note that there is a certain limitation on the names of our projects in the event that we adopt this strategy: They should have names that are legitimate module names, so a program called convert-incidents.py can't have a test like this composed for it since import convert-occurrences isn't substantial since hyphens are not lawful in Python identifiers. (It is conceivable to get around this, yet the most effortless arrangement is to utilize program filenames that are additionally substantial module names, for instance, supplanting hyphens with underscores.)

The structure appeared here—make a test suite, include at least one experiments or test suites, run the general test suite, and yield the outcomes—is regular of unittest-based tests. Whenever run, this specific model delivers the accompanying yield:

...

Ran 3 tests in 0.244s

OK

<unittest._TextTestResult run=3 errors=0 failures=0>

Each time an experiment is executed a period is yield (subsequently the three time frames toward the start of the yield), at that point a line of hyphens, and afterward the test synopsis. (Normally, there is significantly more yield if any tests fall flat.)

On the off chance that we are trying to have separate tests (regularly one for every star gram and module we need to test), at that point as opposed to utilizing doctests we may want to straightforwardly utilize the unittest module's highlights—particularly on the off chance that we are utilized to the JUnit way to deal with testing. The unittest module keeps our tests separate from our code—this is especially helpful for bigger undertakings where test journalists and engineers are not really similar individuals. Additionally, unittest unit tests are composed as remain solitary Python modules, so they are not restricted by what we can serenely and reasonably compose inside a docstring.

The unittest module characterizes four key ideas. A test installation is the term used to depict the code important to set up a test (and to tear it down, that is, tidy up, a short time later). Ordinary models are making an information document for the test to utilize and toward the end erasing the information record and the resultant yield record. A testsuite is a gathering of experiments and an experiment is the fundamental unit of testing—testsuites are accumulations of experiments or of other test suites—we'll see handy instances of these instantly. A test sprinter is an item that executes at least one test suites.

Commonly, a test suite is made by making a subclass of unittest.TestCase, where every strategy that has a name starting with "test" is an experiment. In the event that we need any arrangement to be done, we can do it in a technique called setUp(); comparative ly, for any cleanup we can actualize a strategy called tearDown(). Inside the tests there are various unittest.TestCase techniques that we can utilize, including assertTrue(), assertEqual(), assertAlmostEqual() (helpful for test-ing gliding point numbers), assertRaises(), and some more, including numerous inverses, for example, assertFalse(), assertNotEqual(), failIfEqual(), failUnlessE-qual, etc.

The unittest module is all around archived and has a ton of functionality, however here we will simply give a kind of its utilization by assessing an exceptionally straightforward test suite. The activity was to make an Atomic module which could be utilized as a setting director to guarantee that either the majority of a lot of changes is applied to a rundown, set, or lexicon—or none of them are. The Atomic.py module gave for instance arrangement utilizes 30 lines of code to actualize the Atomic class, and has around 100 lines of module doctests. We will make the test_Atomic.py module to supplant the doctests with unittest tests so we would then be able to erase the doctests and leave Atomic.py free of any code aside from that expected to give its functionality.

Prior to plunging into composing the test module, we have to consider what tests are required. We should test three various types of information type: records, sets, and lexicons. For records we have to test attaching and embeddings a thing, erasing a thing, and changing a thing's worth. For sets we should test including and disposing of a thing. What's more, for word references we should test embeddings a thing, changing a thing's worth, and erasing a thing. Additionally, we should test that on account of disappointment, none of the progressions are applied.

Fundamentally, testing the various information types is basically the equivalent, so we will just compose the experiments for testing records and leave the others as an activity. The test_Atomic.py module must import both the unittest module and the Atomic module that it is intended to test.

When making unittest records, we ordinarily make modules as opposed to programs, and inside every module we characterize at least one unittest.TestCase subclasses. On account of the test_Atomic.py module, it characterizes a single unittest.TestCase subclass, TestAtomic (which we will audit quickly), and closes with the accompanying two lines:

```
if __name__ == "__main__":
```

```
unittest.main()
```

Thanks to these lines, the module can be run stand-alone. And of course, it could also be imported and run from another test program—something that makes sense if this is just one test suite among many.

If we want to run the test_Atomic.py module from another test program we can write a program that is similar to the one we used to execute doctests using the unittest module. For example:

```
import unittest
```

```
import test_Atomic
```

```
suite = unittest.TestLoader().loadTestsFromTestCase(
test_Atomic.TestAtomic)
```

```python
runner = unittest.TextTestRunner()

print(runner.run(suite))
```

Here, we have created a single suite by telling the unittest module to read the test_Atomic module and to use each of its test*() methods (test_list_success() and test_list_fail() in this example, as we will see in a moment), as test cases.

We will now review the implementation of the TestAtomic class. Unusually for subclasses generally, although not for unittest.TestCase subclasses, there is no need to implement the initializer. In this case we will need a setup method, but not a teardown method. And we will implement two test cases.

```python
def setUp(self):

    self.original_list = list(range(10))
```

We have used the unittest.TestCase.setUp() method to create a single piece of test data.


```python
def test_list_succeed(self):

    items = self.original_list[:]

    with Atomic.Atomic(items) as atomic:

        atomic.append(1999)

        atomic.insert(2, -915)

        del atomic[5]

        atomic[4] = -782
```

```
atomic.insert(0, -9)
```

```
self.assertEqual(items,
```

```
[-9, 0, 1, -915, 2, -782, 5, 6, 7, 8, 9, 1999])
```

This experiment is utilized to test that the majority of a lot of changes to a rundown are accurately applied. The test plays out an affix, an addition in the center, an inclusion toward the start, a cancellation, and a difference in a worth. While in no way, shape or form exhaustive, the test does at any rate spread the rudiments.

The test ought not raise a special case, however on the off chance that it does the unittest.TestCase base class will deal with it by transforming it into a suitable blunder message. Toward the end we expect the things rundown to rise to the exacting rundown incorporated into the test as opposed to the first rundown. The unittest.TestCase.assertEqual() strategy cancompare any two Python objects, however its simplification implies that it can't give especially instructive blunder messages.

From Python 3.1, the unittest.TestCase class has many more methods, includ-ing many data-type-specific assertion methods. Here is how we could write the assertion using Python 3.1:

```
self.assertListEqual(items,
```

```
[-9, 0, 1, -915, 2, -782, 5, 6, 7, 8, 9, 1999])
```

If the lists are not equal, since the data types are known, the unittest module is able to give more precise error information, including where the lists differ.

```
def test_list_fail(self):
```

```
def process():
```

```python
nonlocal items

with Atomic.Atomic(items) as atomic:

atomic.append(1999)

atomic.insert(2, -915)

del atomic[5]

atomic[4] = -782

atomic.poop() # Typo

items = self.original_list[:] self.assertRaises(AttributeError, process)
self.assertEqual(items, self.original_list)
```

To test the disappointment case, that is, the place an exemption is raised while doing nuclear preparing, we should test that the rundown has not been changed and furthermore that a suitable special case has been raised. To check for a special case we utilize the unittest.TestCase.assertRaises() technique, and on account of Python 3.0, wepass it the exemption we hope to get and a callable item that should raise the special case. This powers us to typify the code we need to test, which is the reason we needed to make the procedure() internal function appeared here.

In Python 3.1 the unittest.TestCase.assertRaises() technique can be utilized as a setting director, so we can compose our test in a significantly more normal manner:

```python
def test_list_fail(self):

items = self.original_list[:]

with self.assertRaises(AttributeError):
```

```python
with Atomic.Atomic(items) as atomic:

atomic.append(1999)

atomic.insert(2, -915)

del atomic[5]

atomic[4] = -782

atomic.poop() # Typo

self.assertListEqual(items, self.original_list)
```

Here we have composed the test code legitimately in the test strategy without the requirement for an internal function, rather utilizing unittest.TestCase.assertRaised() as a setting supervisor that anticipates that the code should raise an AttributeError. We have too utilized Python 3.1's unittest.TestCase.assertListEqual() technique toward the end.

As we have seen, Python's test modules are anything but difficult to utilize and are incredibly use-ful, particularly in the event that we use TDD. They additionally have significantly more functionality and fea-tures than have been appeared here—for instance, the capacity to skip tests which is valuable to represent stage contrasts—and they are likewise well record ed. One component that is missing—and which nose and py.test give—is test revelation, in spite of the fact that this element is required to show up in a later Python rendition (maybe as right on time as Python 3.2).

Profiling

On the off chance that a program runs gradually or expends unquestionably more memory than we expect, the issue is regularly because of our selection of calculations or information structures, or because of our doing a wasteful usage. Whatever the purpose behind the issue, it is ideal to discover definitely where the issue lies as opposed to simply assessing our code and attempting to streamline it. Haphazardly advancing can make us acquaint bugs or with accelerate portions of our program that really have no impact on the program's general execution on the grounds that the upgrades are not in spots where the translator invests a large portion of its energy.

Prior to going further into profiling, it is significant a couple of Python programming propensities that are anything but difficult to learn and apply, and that are useful for execution. None of the methods is Python-variant explicit, and every one of them are superbly solid Python programming style. To start with, lean toward tuples to records when a read–just succession is required. Second, use generators instead of making enormous tuples or records to repeat over. Third, utilize Python's worked in information structures—dicts, records, and tuples—instead of custom information structures executed in Python, since the inherent ones are for the most part profoundly upgraded. Fourth, when making huge strings out of heaps of little strings, rather than con-catenating the little strings, amass them all in a rundown, and join the rundown of strings into a single string toward the end. Fifth lastly, if an item (counting a function or strategy) is gotten to an enormous number of times utilizing characteristic access (e.g., when getting to a function in a module), or from an information structure, it might be smarter to make and utilize a neighborhood variable that alludes to the article to give quicker access.

Python's standard library gives two modules that are especially valuable when we need to research the exhibition of our code. One of these is the timeit module—this is valuable for timing little bits of Python code, and can beused, for instance, to look at the presentation of at least two usage of a specific function or technique. The other is the cProfile module which canbe used to profile a program's exhibition—it gives a point by point breakdown of call checks and times thus can be utilized to discover execution bottlenecks..

To give a kind of the timeit module, we will take a gander at a little model. Assume we have three functions, function_a(), function_b(), and function_c(), all of which play out a similar calculation, yet each utilizing an alternate calculation. On the off chance that we put every one of these functions into a module (or import them), we can run them utilizing the timeit module to perceive how they look at. Here's the code that we can use toward the finish of our module:

```
if __name__ == "__main__":

repeats = 1000

for function in ("function_a", "function_b", "function_c"):

t = timeit.Timer("{0}(X, Y)".format(function),

"from __main__ import {0}, X, Y".format(function))

sec = t.timeit(repeats) / repeats

print("{function}() {sec:.6f} sec".format(**locals()))
```

The main contention given to the timeit.Timer() constructor is the code we need to execute and time, as a string. Here, the first run through around the circle, the string is "function_a(X, Y)". The subsequent contention is discretionary; again it is a string to be executed, this time before the code to be coordinated to give some arrangement. Here we have imported from the __main__ (i.e., this) module the function we need to test, in addition to two factors that are passed as information (X and Y), and that are accessible as worldwide factors in the module. We could simply have imported the function and information from an alternate module.

At the point when the timeit.Timer item's timeit() technique is called, it will initially execute the constructor's subsequent contention—on the off chance that there was one—to set things up, and afterward it will execute the constructor's first contention—and time to what extent the execution takes. The timeit.Timer.timeit() strategy's arrival worth is the time taken right away, as a buoy. As a matter of course, the timeit() technique rehashes 1 million times and returns the absolute seconds for every one of these executions, however in this partic-ular case we required just 1 000 rehashes to give us helpful outcomes, so we determined the recurrent check unequivocally. In the wake of timing each function we separate the aggregate by the quantity of rehashes to get its mean (normal) execution time and print the function's name and execution time on the support.

function_a() 0.001618 sec

function_b() 0.012786 sec

function_c() 0.003248 sec

In the example, function_a() is the fastest—at least with the input data we used. In some situations—for example, where performance canvary considerably depending on the input data—we might have to test each function with multiple sets of input data to cover a representative set of cases and then compare the total or average execution times.

It isn't constantly helpful to instrument our code to get timings, thus the timeit module gives a method for timing code from the direction line. Forexample, to time function_a() from the MyModule.py module, we would enter the accompanying in the reassure: python3 - m timeit - n 1000 - s "from MyModule importfunction_a, X, Y" "function_a(X, Y)". (Of course, for Windows, we should supplant python3 with something like C:\Python31\python.exe.) The - m alternative is for thePython translator and tells it to stack the predetermined module (for this situation timeit) and different choices are taken care of by the timeit module. The - n choice determines the reiteration check, the - s choice indicates the arrangement, and the last contention is the code to execute and time. After the direction has completed it prints its outcomes on the comfort, for instance:

1000 loops, best of 3: 1.41 msec per loop

We can without much of a stretch at that point rehash the planning for the other two functions so we can look at them all.

The cProfile module can likewise be utilized to think about the exhibition of functionsand techniques. What's more, not at all like the timeit module that just gives crude timings, the cProfile module indicates correctly what is being called and to what extent each call takes. Here's the code we would use to look at indistinguishable three functions from previously:

if __name__ == "__main__":

for function in ("function_a", "function_b", "function_c"):

cProfile.run("for i in range(1000): {0}(X, Y)"

.format(function))

We should put the quantity of rehashes inside the code we go to the cPro-file.run() function, yet we don't have to do any arrangement since the module func-tion utilizes reflection to discover the functions and factors we need to utilize. There is no express print() articulation since naturally the cProfile.run() func-tion prints its yield on the reassure. Here are the outcomes for every one of the functions (with some immaterial lines discarded and marginally reformatted to fit the page):

1003 function calls in 1.661 CPU seconds

ncalls tottime percall cumtime percall
filename:lineno(function)

1
0.003
0.003
1.661
1.661
<string>:1(<module>)

1000
1.658
0.002
1.658
0.002
MyModule.py:21(function_a)

1 0.000 0.000 1.661 1.661 {built-in method exec}

5132003 function calls in 22.700 CPU seconds

The ncalls ("number of calls") section records the quantity of calls to the predefined function (recorded in the filename:lineno(function) segment). Review that we re-peated the calls 1 000 times, so we should remember this. The tottime ("complete time") segment records the all out time spent in the function, however barring time spent inside functions called by the function. The first percall section records the normal time of each call to the function (tottime/ncalls). The cumtime ("total time") segment records the time spent in the function and incorporates the time spent inside functions called by the function. The second percall section records the normal time of each call to the function, including functions called by it.

This yield is unmistakably more illuminating than the timeit module's crude timings. We can promptly observe that both function_b() and function_c() use generators that are called in excess of 5 000 times, making them both in any event multiple times more slow than function_a(). Moreover, function_b() calls more functions gen-erally, including a call to the inherent arranged() function, and this makes it twice as delayed as function_c(). Obviously, the timeit() module gave us adequate data to see these distinctions in timing, however the cProfile module enables us to see the subtleties of why the distinctions are there in any case.

Similarly as the timeit module enables us to time code without instrumenting it, so does the cProfile module. Be that as it may, when utilizing the cProfile module from the order line we can't determine precisely what we need executed—it basically executes the given program or module and reports the timings of everything. The order line to utilize is python3 - m cProfileprogramOrModule.py, and the yield created is in a similar configuration as we saw before; here is a concentrate marginally reformatted and with most lines discarded:

10272458

function calls (10272457 primitive calls) in 37.718 CPU secs

ncalls
tottime
percall
cumtime
percall
filename:lineno(function)

1
0.000
0.000
37.718
37.718
<string>:1(<module>)

1 0.7190.719 37.717 37.717 <string>:12(<module>)

1000
1.569
0.002
1.569

0.002
<string>:20(function_a)

1000
0.011
0.000
22.560
0.023
<string>:27(function_b)

5128000
7.078
0.000
7.078
0.000
<string>:28(<genexpr>)

1000
6.510
0.007
12.825
0.013
<string>:35(function_c)

5128000
6.316
0.000
6.316
0.000
<string>:36(<genexpr>)

In the cProfile naming, a *primitive* call is a nonrecursive call.

Using the cProfile module this way could be useful to identify areas that are worth checking further. Now, for example, we can easily see that the function_b() takes a long time to run. How do we explore the details further? We can modify the program by replacing calls to function_b() with a similar code: cProfile.run("function_b()"). Otherwise, we could save the full profile data and check it using the pstats module. To save the profile we must modify our command line slightly: python3 -m cProfile -o*profileDataFile programOrModule*.py. We can then analyze the profile data, for example, by starting IDLE, importing the pstats module, and giving it the saved *profileDataFile*, or by using pstats interactive-ly the console. Now, there's a very simple example of console session that has been tidied up to fit on this page, and with the input marked in bold:

$ python3 -m cProfile -o profile.dat MyModule.py

$ python3 -m pstats

Welcome to the profile statistics browser. % **read profile.dat**

profile.dat% **callers function_b**

Random listing order was used

List reduced from 44 to 1 due to restriction <'function_b'> Function was called by...
ncalls tottime cumtime

<string>:27(function_b) <- 1000 0.011 22.251 <string>:12(<module>)

profile.dat% **callees function_b**

Random listing order was used

List reduced from 44 to 1 due to restriction <'function_b'> Function called...
ncalls tottime cumtime

  <string>:27(function_b) ->

1000
0.005
0.005
built-in method bisect_left

1000
0.001
0.001
built-in method len

1000
15.297
22.234
built-in method sorted

profile.dat% **quit**

Type help to get the rundown of directions, and help pursued by an order name for more data on the direction. For instance, help details will list what contentions can be given to the statscommand. Different instruments are accessible that can give a graphical perception of the profile information, for instance, RunSnakeRun (www.vrplumber.com/programming/runsnakerun), which relies upon the wxPython GUI library.

Utilizing the timeit and cProfile modules we can distinguish zones of our code that may take additional time than anticipated, and utilizing the cProfile module, we can discover precisely where the time is being taken.

Chapter 7: Processes and Threading

Thanks to multicore processors becoming the norm instead of the exception, it is more attractive and more effective than ever before to want to expand the processing pressure so as to get the most out of all the accessible cores. There are two main strategies to expanding the workload. One is to use many processes and the other is to use different threads. This section explains how to use both procedures.

Using multiple processes, that is, running separate programs, has the advantage that each process runs independently. This leaves all the burden of handling concurrency to the underlying operating system. The disadvantage is that communication and data sharing between the invoking program and the separate processes it invokes can be inconvenient. On Unix systems this can be solved by using the exec and fork paradigm, but for cross-platform pro-grams other solutions must be used. The simplest, and the one shown here, is for the invoking program to feed data to the processes it runs and leave them to produce their output independently. A more flexible approach that greatly simplifies two-way communication is to use networking. Of course, in many situations such communication isn't needed—we just need to run one or more other programs from one orchestrating program.

An alternative to handing off work to independent processes is to create a threaded program that distributes work to independent threads of execution. This has the advantage that we can communicate simply by sharing data (providing we ensure that shared data is accessed only by one thread at a time), but leaves the burden of managing concurrency squarely with the programmer. Python provides good support for creating threaded programs, minimizing the work that we must do. Nonetheless, multi-threaded programs are inherently more complex than single-threaded programs and require much more care in their creation and maintenance.

In this chapter's first section we will create two small programs. The first program is called by the user and the second program is invoked by the first program, with the second program called once for every separate method that is required. In the next section we will start by providing a bare-bones intro to threaded programming. Then we will build a threaded application that has an identical functionality as the two from the first section coupled together, to provide a difference between the multiple process and the multiple thread approach. We'll then describe another threaded program, more advanced than the first, that both hands off operate and groups together all the outputs.

Using the Multiprocessing Module

In some situations we already have programs that have the functionality we need but we want to automate their use. We can do this by using Python's sub-process module which provides facilities for running other programs, passingany command-line options we want, and if desired, communicating with them using pipes. We saw one very simple example of this in Chapter 5 when we used the subprocess.call() function to clear the console in a platform-specific way. But we can also use these facilities to create pairs of "parent–child" pro-grams, where the parent program is run by the user and this in turn runs as many instances of the child program as necessary, each with different work to do. It is this approach that we will cover in this section.

In Chapter 3 we demonstrated an extremely straightforward program, grepword.py, that looks for a word determined on the order line in the records recorded after the word. In this area we will build up an increasingly advanced adaptation that can recurse into subdirectories to discover records to peruse and that can assign the work to the same number of discrete kid forms as we like. The yield is only a rundown of filenames (with ways) for those documents that contain the predetermined pursuit word.

The parent program is grepword-p.py and the kid program is grepword-p-child.py. The connection between the two projects when they are being runis demonstrated schematically in Figure 10.1.

The core of grepword-p.py is epitomized by its principle() function, which we will take a gander at in three sections:

```
def main():

child = os.path.join(os.path.dirname(__file__), "grepword-p-child.py")
opts, word, args = parse_options()

filelist = get_files(args, opts.recurse)
```

```python
files_per_process = len(filelist) // opts.count

start, end = 0, files_per_process + (len(filelist) % opts.count) number = 1
```

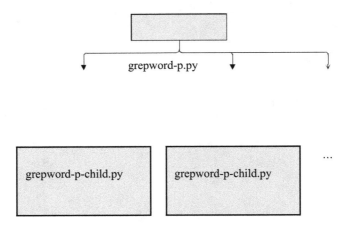

grepword-p.py

grepword-p-child.py   grepword-p-child.py   ...

Parent and child programs

We start by getting the name of the kid program. At that point we get the client's direction line alternatives. The parse_options() function utilizes the optparse module. It restores the picks named tuple which demonstrates whether the program ought to recurse into subdirectories and the tally of what number of procedures to utilize—the default is 7, and the program has a self-assertively picked limit of 20. It additionally restores the word to scan for and the rundown of names (filenames and registry names) given on the order line. The get_files() function restores a rundown of records to be perused.

When we have the data important to play out the assignment we compute what number of records must be given to each procedure to chip away at. The beginning and end factors are utilized to determine the cut of the filelist that will be given to the following kid procedure to deal with. Generally the quantity of documents won't be a definite different of the quantity of procedures, so we increment the quantity of records the principal procedure is given by the rest of. The number variable is utilized only for troubleshooting with the goal that we can see which procedure created each line of yield.

```
pipes = []

while start < len(filelist):

command = [sys.executable, child]

if opts.debug:

command.append(str(number))

pipe = subprocess.Popen(command, stdin=subprocess.PIPE)
```

```python
        pipes.append(pipe)

        pipe.stdin.write(word.encode("utf8") + b"\n")

        for filename in filelist[start:end]:

            pipe.stdin.write(filename.encode("utf8") + b"\n")

        pipe.stdin.close()

        number += 1

        start, end = end, end + files_per_process
```

For each start:end slice of the filelist we create a command list consisting of the Python interpreter (conveniently available in sys.executable), the child pro-gram we want Python to execute, and the command-line options—in this case just the child number if we are debugging. If the child program has a suitable shebang line or file association we could list it first and not bother including the Python interpreter, but we prefer this approach because it ensures that the child program uses the same Python interpreter as the parent program.

When we have the order prepared we make a subprocess.Popen object, speci-fying the direction to execute (as a rundown of strings), and for this situation mentioning to keep in touch with the procedure's standard info. (It is additionally conceivable to peruse a procedure's standard yield by setting a comparable catchphrase contention.) We at that point compose the pursuit word pursued by a newline and after that each document in the significant cut of the record list. The subprocess module peruses and composes bytes, not strings, however the procedures it makes consistently expect that the bytes got from sys.stdin are strings in the neighborhood encoding— regardless of whether the bytes we have sent utilize an alternate en-coding, for example, UTF-8 which we have utilized here. We will perceive how to get around this irritating issue without further ado. When the word and the rundown of documents have been kept in touch with the youngster procedure, we close its standard info and proceed onward.

It isn't carefully important to hold a reference to each procedure (the pipe variable gets bounce back to another subprocess.Popen object each time through the circle), since each procedure runs autonomously, however we add every one to a rundown with the goal that we can make them interruptible. Likewise, we don't assemble the outcomes, yet rather we let each procedure compose its outcomes to the reassure voluntarily. This implies the yield from various procedures could be interleaved. (You will find the opportunity to abstain from interleaving in the activities.)

```
while pipes:


    pipe = pipes.pop()


    pipe.wait()
```

When every one of the procedures have begun we sit tight for every kid procedure to wrap up. This isn't basic, yet on Unix-like frameworks it guarantees that we are come back to the comfort brief when every one of the procedures are done (else, we should press Enter when they are altogether wrapped up). Another advantage of holding up is that on the off chance that we intrude on the program (e.g., by squeezing Ctrl+C), every one of the procedures that are as yet running will be hindered and will end with an uncaught KeyboardInterrupt special case—on the off chance that we didn't hold up the primary program would complete (and in this manner not be interruptible), and the youngster procedures would proceed (except if slaughtered by an execute program or an assignment chief).

Aside from the remarks and imports, here is the finished grepword-p-child.py program. We will take a gander at the program in two sections—with two variants of the initial segment, the first for any Python 3.x rendition and the second for Python 3.1 or later forms:

```
BLOCK_SIZE = 8000
```

```
number = "{0}: ".format(sys.argv[1]) if len(sys.argv) == 2 else ""
stdin = sys.stdin.buffer.read()

lines = stdin.decode("utf8", "ignore").splitlines()
```

```
word = lines[0].rstrip()
```

The program begins by setting the number string to the given number or to an empty string if we are not debugging. Since the program is running as a child process and the subprocess module only reads and writes binary data and always uses the local encoding, we must read sys.stdin's underlying buffer of binary data and perform the decoding ourselves.

Once we have read the binary data, we decode it into a Unicode string and split it into lines. The child process then reads the first line, since this contains the search word.

Here are the lines that are different for Python 3.1:

```
sys.stdin = sys.stdin.detach()
```

```
stdin = sys.stdin.read()
```

```
lines = stdin.decode("utf8", "ignore").splitlines()
```

Python 3.1 provides the sys.stdin.detach() method that returns a binary file object. We then read in all the data, decode it into Unicode using the encoding of our choice, and then split the Unicode string into lines.

```
for filename in lines[1:]:

filename = filename.rstrip()

previous = ""

try:

with open(filename, "rb") as fh:

while True:

current = fh.read(BLOCK_SIZE)
```

```python
    if not current:
        break
    current = current.decode("utf8", "ignore")
    if (word in current or
        word in previous[-len(word):] +
        current[:len(word)]):
        print("{0} {1}".format(number, filename))
        break
    if len(current) != BLOCK_SIZE:
        break
    previous = current
except EnvironmentError as err:
    print("{0} {1}".format(number, err))
```

All the lines after the first are filenames (with paths). For each one we open the relevant file, read it, and print its name if it contains the search word. It is possible that some of the files might be very large and this could be a problem, especially if there are 20 child processes running concurrently, all reading big files. We handle this by perusing each record in squares, keeping the past square read to guarantee that we don't miss situations when the main event of the hunt word happens to fall crosswise over two squares. Another advantage of perusing in squares is that if the pursuit word shows up from the get-go in the record we can complete with the document without having perused everything, since all we care about is whether the word is in the document, not where it shows up inside the document.

The documents are perused in double mode, so we should change over each square to a string be-fore we can look through it, since the inquiry word is a string. We have expected that every one of the documents utilize the UTF-8 encoding, yet this is in all likelihood wrong sometimes. An increasingly advanced program would attempt to decide the genuine encoding and after that nearby and revive the document utilizing the right encoding. As we noted in Chapter 2, in any event two Python bundles for naturally identifying a document's encoding are accessible from the Python Package Index, pypi.python.org/pypi. (It may entice to interpret the inquiry word into a bytes item and contrast bytes and bytes, yet that approach isn't dependable since certain characters have more than one legitimate UTF-8 portrayal.)

The subprocess module offers much more functionality than we have expected to use here, including the capacity to give counterparts to shell backquotes and shell pipelines, and to the os.system() and generate functions.

www.ingramcontent.com/pod-product-compliance
Lightning Source LLC
Chambersburg PA
CBHW071238050326
40690CB00011B/2172